L.E.E R. UPDIKE

ABOUT THE AUTHOR

Lee Updike was born in White Fox in rural northern Saskatchewan in 1932. As a youth, he worked the family farm, ran a trapline, and worked in sawmills and in the bush. Updike started boxing as a teenager and pursued a boxing career until his early twenties. Thereafter, he worked in manufacturing and sales while upgrading his education, particularly in commercial art. While in his early thirties, Updike began freelance illustrating, specializing in drawing and painting the Native peoples of early Canada. Several books have featured Updike's illustrations, and his Indian artwork has been displayed in Canadian museums and galleries.

In the 1970s, Lee Updike hearkened ' and laid aside pen and brush to devote twe Christian ministry. Lee and his wife, Beverly, li where Lee is active in drawing, painting, and v

PRICE: $16.95 (3559/se)

EDGE of the WILDERNESS

GROWING UP IN THE NORTH

Lee Updike

FIFTH
HOUSE

Cover and interior design by Articulate Eye Design
Edited by Erin Creasey
Copyedited by Meaghan Craven
Proofread by Alex Frazer-Harrison

The publisher gratefully acknowledges the support of The Canada Council for the Arts and the Department of Canadian Heritage. We acknowledge the financial support of the Government of Canada through the Book Publishing Industry Development Program (BPIDP) for our publishing activities.

 Canada Council   Conseil des Arts
for the Arts   du Canada

Printed in Canada by Friesens

04 05 06 07 08/ 5 4 3 2 1

First published in the United States in 2004

National Library of Canada Cataloguing in Publication

Updike, Lee R., 1932-
Edge of the wilderness : growing up in the north / Lee Updike.
ISBN 1-894856-35-X

Fifth House Ltd.
A Fitzhenry & Whiteside Company
Calgary, Alberta, Canada
T2S 2S5
1-800-387-9776
www.fitzhenry.ca

Fitzhenry & Whiteside
121 Harvard Avenue, Suite 2
1511-1800 4 St. SW
Allston, MA 02134

In memory of my mom and dad,
Ryburn and Mary Updike.

They faced the hardships of life with calm courage
and did the best they could with what they had.

Contents

The White Fox River runs high and wild in the spring.

Preface

Edge of the Wilderness is a work that has taken a lifetime to get down on paper. It began as a series of short stories about my early life in the bush of northern Saskatchewan. As the stories began to see publication in various magazines, I was encouraged to enlarge the series and bring it together in book form.

This collection of stories is part biography, part history, and part reminiscence about life in a different world. Though the stories are arranged as relating chapters, they are, nevertheless, each a separate story. The first twenty-one stories progress chronologically as I grow from age five to age twenty. The final two describe experiences that occurred in 1957, after I had left the north and returned for an extended visit.

Some names used in the narrative are fictitious but characters and events are real.

The medium used in the illustrations is graphite (except for "Lost in the Bush," which is India ink). Pencil on paper seemed to best represent an unsophisticated people in a less complicated, black and white age. The photographs lend a certain personal and historic perspective. Some are very old and faded, dating back as far as 1916.

There are times I am deeply stirred as I reflect on those years. Sometimes I'm amazed. Sometimes I'm sad. Sometimes I'm encouraged. Sometimes I just sit back and have a good laugh. My hope is that those who peruse these pages might be stirred in some way, too.

Lee Updike

Acknowledgements

This book would not have come into being without the wholehearted support and encouragement of my wife, Beverly. She spent much time alone while I devoted hours to the keyboard and the drawing table.

My sons, Larry and Dan, and my daughter, Janet, offered unflagging encouragement.

My sister, Jean, and brothers, Harley and Dale, were supportive. Dale, especially, provided valuable perspective.

I must also acknowledge the vital contribution made by a number of relatives and friends from long ago. Klaus Peters, a close friend for nearly sixty years, is certainly among them. I also want to make special mention of three men who appear repeatedly in the stories. The first is Charlie Vivian, who worked for my dad and lived with our family until I was about seven; Charlie was the big brother I needed. The second is Uncle Jake, my mom's youngest brother. He had a soft spot in his heart for his sister's kid; it made a difference. And finally, the third is Fred Culhane, my hunting, fishing, and trapping partner. He taught me the left jab and a whole lot more. I wonder what story my early life would tell if Charlie, Uncle Jake, and Fred had not shared of their lives with a lonely kid growing up on the edge of the wilderness.

There was no way to predict the joy and pain that my friend Shorty would bring.

A Friend Named Shorty

I LIKE TO THINK MY LIFE BEGAN WHEN I MET SHORTY. Although I was already five when Dad got him for me, my recollections of life on the farm in northern Saskatchewan where I grew up are unclear before that time.

I remember our first meeting well. I was playing in the back-yard when some neighbours dropped by. Almost immediately Dad called me into the house. I entered the front door timidly, and there he was, standing in the middle of the kitchen.

"Son," said Dad, "meet your new dog!"

Surprised and overwhelmed, I was speechless for a moment. I wanted to run up to the little newcomer but was afraid he would either run away, or chase after me. Not knowing what to do, I climbed into a nearby chair.

"Don't be afraid," Mom said, "he's just little, too."

The puppy started toward my chair. His little toenails made soft clicking sounds on the cheap linoleum. I pulled my bare feet up and out of reach when he came near. He looked up at me with his big, brown, happy eyes. His stubby tail wagged vigorously.

Cautiously, I reached down and touched his soft fur. He licked my hand, and the miracle that can happen between a boy and a dog touched us there. From that moment on we were lifetime friends.

"Dad," I asked, "is he the family's dog?"

"Well," Dad replied with a grin, "he's the family's dog in some ways, but mostly he's just your dog."

I hugged my new dog with joy. What a special day it was! Life was just beginning, and now it was going to be a lot more fun. But there was no way to predict the joy and pain that my friend Shorty would bring.

The little puppy was quite striking. He was totally white except for a coal-black head. His ears were erect and pointed. His tail was short. He was playful and enthusiastic but not yappy.

The whole family chipped in with suggestions to help me choose a name but nothing seemed just right, until Dad said "I once had a dog named Shorty. Your dog is short, his hair is short, his tail is short; what do you think of Shorty for a name?"

"I like it! I like it!" I shouted. So we named the family dog—but mostly my dog—Shorty.

Just like his owner, Shorty had a lot of growing up and a lot of learning to do. His first lesson was "no more puddles on the floor." Then "don't leave the yard," and "don't chase the chickens." That was a tough one, as was "don't bark at the cattle."

We soon discovered that Shorty was exceptionally bright. His happy enthusiasm pleased the whole family. Most importantly, he was a special friend to me. I talked to him a lot. He would listen intently as though straining to understand, and I believe he often did understand. He always seemed to sense what I was feeling, as good friends usually do.

Late the following winter, our hired man Charlie introduced Shorty to working with the cattle. One day when we were putting the stock in the barn, several cows lagged behind, so Charlie sent Shorty to bring them in. The little dog was a natural; he knew what to do instinctively, and he enjoyed the work so much he wouldn't quit. Charlie called him off repeatedly. Nothing doing, he was too busy chasing cows. In exasperation, Charlie hurled a baseball-sized chunk of frozen cow manure in Shorty's direction. The unwholesome missile sped through the frigid air as if it were laser-guided. It struck my little dog in the head and dropped him instantly.

Charlie and I ran to the fallen animal. Charlie's powerful strides covered the distance quickly, while I struggled to keep up in snow to my knees. I cried in anguish at the sight that greeted us. Shorty's small body lay half covered in snow. Blood from a cut over his left eye seemed redder than red as it congealed in the snow.

"Charlie," I wailed, "you killed my dog!"

"No," Charlie replied, deeply concerned, "he ain't dead, he's still breathing. Let's take him to the house, your dad will know what to do."

Charlie scooped up the unconscious pup and took off for the house, his gum rubbers kicking up showers of snow. Again I struggled behind, bawling my eyes out. In my six-year-old mind, the little dog I had come to love so much was already dead.

By the time I reached the house Charlie was already inside, and Dad was examining Shorty.

"He's going to be okay, Son," Dad said, seeing my tears. "See, he's beginning to come to. He'll have a lump on his head, and he might not feel so good for a while, but he's going to be all right."

Shorty did indeed have a large swelling over his eye, and he whimpered a little, but in a couple of hours he was fairly happy and back to normal.

Later that week, Charlie and I took Shorty out to work with the cattle again. This time when Charlie called him off he withdrew immediately. "He sure learned his lesson," Charlie observed.

"But you ain't going to chuck manure at him any more, are you, Charlie?" I asked with concern.

"Heck, no!" Charlie laughed, "I guess I learned my lesson, too."

In time, Shorty became an extremely effective cattle dog. He didn't look the part, but he always found a way to get the job done.

When I was seven, it became one of my summer chores to round up the cows in the pasture and bring them into the corral for evening milking. I always took Shorty with me. He was a tremendous help when some of the cows didn't want to leave the pasture, or when they weren't interested in paying attention to a seven-year-old.

If a cow tried to kick Shorty, he would drop to the ground while the dangerous hoof sailed overhead. Then, before the leg could be brought forward, he would dart in and sink his teeth into the other leg. Our stock soon learned to respect the little white dog and to respond quickly when he came to fetch them.

One summer we pastured a neighbour's Black Angus cow. Ol' Maggie was a mean one. She wanted nothing to do with being rounded up by a kid, so I let Shorty deal with her. That old black rebel kicked, bellowed, and charged. She refused to be herded anywhere so Shorty simply ran ahead of her—and she unwittingly chased him all the way to the corral.

As Maggie entered the corral gate, Shorty drifted around behind her, then slipped forward, lightning fast, and imprinted a firm message into the heel of each hind leg, several times. Within a few days, even Ol' Maggie filed quietly into the corral with the other cows at milking time.

One evening during a downpour, I decided I didn't want to go for the cows. I knelt before my dog and said, "Shorty, go fetch the cows for me."

He studied my face for a moment then loped off toward the pasture. Twenty minutes later the cattle were calmly winding their way into the corral, Shorty trotting proudly behind them.

After that, the dog could handle the chore without supervision, and I never needed to go for the cows myself, unless I wanted to. Often, Shorty would bring the herd in without being told and always at just the right time.

Shorty was very protective of our farmyard. He never bit anyone, but he was suspicious of strangers and strange dogs. Late one October, our neighbour Mr. Sparrow brought his circular saw outfit over to saw our firewood logs into stove-sized blocks. Mr. Sparrow also brought his big dog, Rex. Shorty did not like this at all; Rex was an ugly black mongrel, twice the size of him. I was afraid the dogs would fight, and I didn't like the odds. "Mr. Sparrow," I said, "I'm scared our dogs are going to fight."

"I don't care if they do," he laughed, "my Rex can take care of himself."

Before I could reply, they were at it! Growling savagely, the dogs leaped at each other. Suddenly, the bigger dog lunged high. Shorty dropped to the ground and swapped ends as Rex overshot his target. In a flash, Shorty slid forward, grabbed the black dog's front paw, and crunched.

Big Rex let out a big howl and tried to disengage from the battle. Blood spurted from two ugly holes in his paw. He tried to hobble away on three legs, but Shorty pursued relentlessly, slashing at his shaggy rump.

I rushed into the fray and held my dog back while the defeated Rex limped out of the yard. I held the little gladiator until he stopped trembling and calmed down. Then I put him in the garage.

I went to Mr. Sparrow and said with childish innocence, "Rex will be safe now, Mr. Sparrow, I locked my dog in the garage."

Mr. Sparrow's mouth puckered sourly and he stomped away without a word. He was followed by a chorus of loud guffaws from the wood-sawing crew. Nobody laughed harder than Charlie.

As great a companion as Shorty was, he was not a good hunting dog. He was too full of fun and enthusiasm, and he was so protective of me that if any animal appeared he immediately went on the attack.

One wet spring there was an unusual amount of run-off water filling the ditches and even flowing over our garden. I noticed something swimming in a dead-furrow in the garden and ran out to investigate. I startled a muskrat that had travelled overland from the creek. Muskrats are fairly timid, but when cornered they will fight. This muskrat apparently felt threatened by me. He scurried out of the water and jumped at my leg. Fortunately, I was wearing high rubber boots and his teeth did not penetrate to my ankle.

Shorty was incensed. In an instant, he seized the furry brown intruder and snapped its neck. Dad skinned it and got two dollars for the pelt from the Hudson's Bay.

Shorty patrolled our farmyard like a miniature police dog. In spring, when circling hawks attempted to swoop down and prey on young chickens, Shorty would drive them off with frenzied barking. He was vigilant in guarding the henhouse against prowling weasels and skunks, and if a fox or coyote came near he would raise such a ruckus that they would soon retreat.

One Saturday, Shorty was away from the yard for quite a while. As soon as he returned, I knew he was in trouble. He didn't come to me, but slunk straight to Dad with his head down. I rushed over and saw that his whole muzzle was strangely white. "Dad," I cried out, "what's wrong with him?"

"Quills," Dad replied. "He's tangled with a porcupine out there and he's loaded with quills."

Shorty lay motionless at Dad's feet, whimpering softly. "Can you help him, Dad?" I asked tearfully.

"This will be very difficult," Dad said gravely. "I've never seen a dog this full of quills before, but I'll do everything I can. I'll need the tin snips and the needle-nosed pliers." I raced to the shop and brought Dad the tools.

"You know, Son," he said, "your mother has a lot of garden that needs hoeing. I think it would be best for you and your dog if you worked in the garden while I work at getting these quills out."

I petted Shorty for a moment and then headed reluctantly for the garden. I worked hard, trying to keep my mind off my dog, but nothing helped. I was worried sick.

Porcupine quills are tiny tubular shafts, about two inches long. The business end has a needle-sharp, barbed point. The other end is blunt but sealed. Through experience, Dad found that if the blunt end is snipped off, the shaft becomes more flexible and less likely to break off and leave the point embedded.

Shorty had quills in his tongue and the roof of his mouth. It took an hour and a half to get them all. He was not in good shape when the ordeal was finally over. He just lay by the house and wouldn't move. It was several days before he fully recovered. I never liked porcupines much after that.

One spring, rats invaded our farm. Although they worked undercover at first, soon the place was overrun with them. Rats are a curse to any farming operation. The little varmints seem to possess diabolical cunning minds. As if by magic, they can find or chew their way into grain bins or other food storage. They do incredible damage, not just to what they eat or pack away, but also to what they contaminate with their excretions.

The rats headquartered in the free space beneath the heavy planking of the barn floor. At first Dad was concerned, then annoyed, and then just plain angry. We picked off a few with the .22, caught a couple in steel traps, and put down lots of poison. But nothing really worked—they flourished.

When I was at school one day, Dad got so fed up with the rats he took up the barn floor in an attempt to get at them. He started at the east wall, one plank at a time. Of course, Shorty was there, eager to help. The rats began to scurry and squeal as they realized that what had been their stronghold was now a deadly trap. Tension mounted as each plank was removed. When Dad flipped over the last one and threw it aside, dozens of rats were exposed. Their only escape was the main door. Dad quickly positioned himself at the door and smacked a few would-be escapees with the shovel. "After that," he reported, "it was all Shorty!"

When I got home from school, I helped Dad replace the barn floor. As we worked he told me the rat story. "I never saw an animal move as fast as that dog of yours," Dad said. "He was everywhere at once, and he seemed to anticipate every move the rats might make. He'd grab a rat and snap its spine with one shake of his head, then he'd grab the next one. It was over in minutes and not one escaped. The dog is dynamite on rats! He's terrific!" Dad was obviously pleased and excited.

We were both really proud of Shorty. I called him into the barn. We petted him and told him what a great dog he was. He was so happy he jumped around like a young puppy. Dad and I felt like doing the same thing—we never had rats on the farm again.

As the years passed, my life became progressively busier. I was operating tractors at eight, hauling grain at eleven, and running combines at fourteen. Because Dad was chronically ill, I worked our farm, worked for neighbouring farmers, logged in the bush, worked in saw mills, and ran a trapline in winter. In addition, my trapping partner, Fred Culhane, became my boxing coach. As my activities increased, I saw less and less of my dog.

When I was sixteen, Shorty was eleven, old for an outdoor dog in northern Saskatchewan in the 1940s. At times winter temperatures hovered around forty below zero for a week or two at a time. The years, especially the winters, had taken their toll on my dog. He was crippled with arthritis and endured much pain. To make matters worse, he hated to be inside, even in the barn.

I shared my concern with Dad that September. "I'm really worried about Shorty," I said, "I know he'll never survive another winter, and he seems to be in so much pain. It just isn't fair."

"He's been a wonderful dog," Dad replied, "and he deserves better than to suffer like this and to freeze to death alone some winter night."

We left it at that, but I knew Dad felt the same way I did about Shorty. I also realized that since Shorty was my dog, the troubles of his life were my responsibility. It weighed heavily on me.

For the next couple of weeks I spent a lot of time with Shorty. I talked to him and stroked his coarse fur. I talked about all the great times we'd had over the years and how I felt about what was happening to him. As always, he looked up into my face and seemed to understand.

One beautiful autumn Saturday, Mom, Dad, and my brothers left to spend the afternoon in town. Shorty was lying in the warm sand of the driveway, some distance from the house. As soon as the family left, I sat with my old friend for a long time. We said our goodbyes. He licked my hand and I remembered that special day eleven years earlier when a fluffy little puppy licked the hand of an excited five-year-old. I cried.

I went into the house and stood before what we called "the gun wall." Nine rifles hung there. I took down the .25–35 Savage, a fine and extremely accurate rifle. I left the house through the back door, went around to the north side, aligned the sights quickly and squeezed the trigger. And so it was that a remarkable life came to its conclusion in one fraction of a second.

I thrust the rifle aside and wept bitterly for a long time. I wept because even good things have to end, because life always has death attached to it, and because, at age sixteen, the responsibilities of a friendship are sometimes just too much to handle. I wept because of my dog.

After a while, I took the shovel and dug a small grave under a pine tree in the bush north of the house; there I laid my friend to rest. I selected some flowering iris bulbs from Mom's garden and built a flowerbed over the grave.

Some folks say time heals. Over the years, I have come to believe it is God who heals; He just takes time to finish His work. In any case, the sorrow in my heart lifted after some time, leaving only the many good memories of a very special dog.

No one has lived on our old farm for years. Even the buildings are long gone. But, about thirty yards north of where the house once stood, there is a gnarled old Jack pine, and every year at that spot flowering irises still appear: an enduring memorial to a friend named Shorty.

The Chickadee Hunter

ONE AUTUMN DAY, WHEN I WAS NEARLY SIX, my Dad made me my very own slingshot. He cut a willow crotch, attached some strips of rubber from an old inner tube, and fashioned a stone pocket from a piece of soft leather. I was very happy with the little catapult, and it soon became my most prized possession.

There was one major difficulty with my new weapon, however. I just couldn't hit anything with it. I went to Dad with my problem, and he explained that it was just a matter of time and lots of practice. He assured me that soon I would get the hang of it and be able to shoot accurately.

Wildlife was plentiful around our farm, and I aspired to one day be a skilful hunter like my dad. Among the trees near the farmhouse I often stalked imaginary deer and bears with my slingshot. Once I scared a squirrel, but not very badly; my accuracy did not seem to be improving.

One grey morning, I strode out to my hunting ground about twenty paces north of the house and found the trees full of chickadees. They were busy and cheerful, and the soft music of their songs filled the autumn air.

I was captivated by the little visitors. But it came to me that the chickadees were wild game, and I was a well-armed hunter.

I loaded a small stone into the pocket of my sling and, aiming in the general direction of the nearest feathered group, I fired my weapon. To my amazement, the stone lazily sailed upward and struck an unsuspecting bird in the centre of his grey breast.

At the moment of impact I was elated. For the first time, I had actually hit something! But, as the tiny creature came fluttering and spinning to the ground, my joy quickly leaked away.

I rushed over to find the bird struggling and gasping on the brown grass. I picked him up and held him in my hand. His limbs twitched, then the little black eyes closed and the black-capped head fell back. A shiver passed through the tiny body—then, nothing. He was dead and I knew it. "Don't be dead," I cried. "Don't be dead! I didn't mean it, honest. Please don't be dead." Death is final, even for a chickadee, and this small feathered creature surely was dead.

Heartbroken, I stood and cried under the Jack pines. Tears splashed over my worn brown running shoes. I was grief-stricken over the casualty and guilt-stricken about what I had done. I felt that this must have been the most wicked of all crimes.

I noticed that I still held my slingshot. I flung it to the ground. "I ain't never going to shoot that ol' thing again!" I sobbed. "And I ain't never going to kill anything again, either." I felt like my whole life was over.

I decided that I had to confess. Slowly and mournfully, I made my way to the house, still clutching the dead bird. Dad was not home so I spilled the whole story to Mom. "Mom," I cried, "there are chickadees everywhere out there. I shot up at them with my slingshot and I hit this one. I wished him not to die but he just died anyway. I shot him with my slingshot, Mom, and I killed him dead, and I don't know what to do."

Mom knelt down and examined the bird. "Well, I'm afraid he's dead all right," she said. "It was an accident though, wasn't it?" she asked. "I mean, you really couldn't hit anything with that slingshot, could you?"

"I never hit anything before," I sniffed. "But Mom, I killed him dead."

Mom consoled me. "It's sad that the little bird is dead, but you didn't mean to harm it," she said. "It was an accident. Sometimes accidents just happen. I'm sure you'll be very careful with your slingshot after this, too, won't you?"

I assured her that if I ever used my slingshot again I would be very careful.

"Dad always says we should never hurt good birds. What's Dad going to say?" I asked tearfully.

"Dad was once a small boy," she replied, "and he will understand that you didn't mean to hurt the chickadee."

"But Mom, what about the other birds?" I asked sadly. "They all saw what I did and I bet they all hate me."

"No, no," Mom assured me, "the other birds have all seen you with your slingshot before, so they'll understand that it was an accident. I'll tell you what. You take the shovel and bury this little bird out under the trees. That would be a kind thing to do. All the birds will see you and maybe they'll feel better about their friend. I bet you'll feel better, too."

I dragged the shovel out to the trees and dug a hole between the roots of a big pine, then placed the chickadee in the hole so he looked comfortable. I covered him with the soft earth and formed a little mound over him. I stood beside the miniature gravesite and took off my cap. "Little bird," I said, "I'm real sorry I killed you. I didn't mean to." It seemed inadequate, but I didn't know what else to say.

There was lots of activity in the pine trees that towered overhead. Small grey, black, and white figures continued to bustle about in the branches, seemingly unconcerned about the funeral of their comrade.

I stood very still and watched the chickadees for a while. They seemed to twitter louder than ever, singing "Dee, dee, dee." I thought they were telling me everything was all right. Several of the tiny birds fluttered down to branches that were only a few feet away. "They don't hate me, and they're not scared, either," I said. "Mom was right, they must feel better, and now I feel better, too!"

I cried, "I shot him with my slingshot, Mom, and I killed him dead."

The Rifle

THE MOMENT I SAW THEM, I WAS EXCITED! There were a hundred, maybe, well, ten or twelve at least. They scurried around pecking at the ripe, low-bush cranberries that grew in profusion under the Jack pines.

They were beautiful—their markings were striking and bold, yet they blended perfectly with the surrounding grass and bushes. I had come upon a flock of spruce grouse on my way home from school one fall afternoon. Although many decades have passed, I remember that day when I was seven like it was yesterday.

Our farm was situated on the southern edge of a vast forest. Because we were poor, Dad often shot wild game of all kinds for the family larder, so my first thought when I discovered the birds was that I must run and tell Dad. He would grab his .22, I would show him where the grouse were, and, as sure as you're a foot high, my dad would shoot a bunch of those grouse.

I raced the half mile home and ran breathlessly into the house. "Mom! Mom!" I shouted. "Where's Dad?"

"Dad won't be home till suppertime," Mom replied. "My word, you're excited! What is it?"

"There're a whole bunch of spruce hens just out the road. On our property, too!" I said. "If Dad was here, he'd shoot some."

"Yes, I'm sure he would," Mom replied.

At that moment a bold thought came to me. "Mom," I said, "why don't I take Dad's rifle and shoot some of those grouse?"

"Oh no," Mom said, her brows furrowing.

"But Mom," I persisted, "I can shoot straight, and I know how to handle guns safely. Dad's been teaching me."

"But you are too young, and your Dad isn't here. The guns are his business, not mine," Mom said firmly. "I could go with you, but I've got a canner full of blueberries on the stove and I can't leave the house."

I was suddenly taken with the notion of going to shoot grouse with Dad's .22 rifle. I presented my case to Mom as eloquently as I could. "We need the meat," I said. "Anyway, maybe they've all flown away by now; what harm could there be?"

Mom seemed to be weakening a little, so I introduced my strongest argument. "Dad would trust me. Dad would let me go."

"Maybe he would at that," she conceded. "And I must be out of my mind, because I'm going to let you go. There are conditions, though. You never carry the rifle loaded. You only load when you're going to shoot. You make sure nothing is in line with your target before you pull the trigger. You don't go off our property. And, you come right home." Mom was very stern as she made me promise to meet all her conditions. "Be very careful," she admonished. Then, smiling, she said, "Go and get us a spruce hen for supper."

I was elated. I took Dad's .22 off the wall, handling it with reverence. I put a few cartridges in my pocket from the box Dad kept in a kitchen drawer. Then I sped down the bush road, hoping fervently that the quarry was still there. I was very excited. This was my first solo hunt with a rifle.

I had little difficulty locating the flock. Spruce grouse are not nearly as wary of man as their relatives the prairie chicken and the ruffed grouse. This was definitely in my favour.

I watched from a distance as I sat on a log and tried to make myself calm. Dad taught me that it's impossible to hold your rifle steady and shoot straight if you're puffing from exertion or too excited. I crept behind some bushes and moved closer, and closer still, until I was certain I was well within range. I carefully loaded the rifle and, resting the barrel on the limb of a sapling, took careful aim and fired. The nearest bird toppled over and began flapping its wings jerkily. The rest of the flock burst into noisy flight but soon settled to the ground again about thirty yards away.

I picked up the dead grouse and began to stalk the flock

again. I replaced the spent cartridge when I had finally wriggled close enough for another shot. This time it was a clean miss. In fact, there were three or four misses, and I had to stalk the birds repeatedly.

At last, the second grouse toppled over, and finally, a third one. The third bird flopped about so violently I feared his wound was not fatal and that he might escape. Having used my last bullet and not really knowing what to do, I struck the bird's head to the ground with the rifle butt. Suddenly, there was a sickening crack—I had cracked the stock of my dad's rifle.

I groaned in anguish. How could I have done such a stupid thing? I wanted Dad to be proud of me, I thought, and now I've ruined his rifle. Because of this, I'll be a grown-up before Dad lets me have a rifle of my own.

I walked home slowly. My two hands symbolized a fierce inner conflict. In my left hand was the evidence of my hunting prowess: three spruce hens. My right hand held what was to me the proof of my total failure as a human being: my dad's rifle with a cracked stock.

As I entered the yard, Shorty welcomed me with friendly barking. Mom came outside. Seeing the three birds, she was surprised and excited. "Son, you got three!" she exclaimed. "You're a hunter just like your dad. Will he be pleased!"

Mom noticed my troubled countenance and asked what was wrong.

"Mom," I said sadly, "I cracked the stock of Dad's rifle, and I'm afraid he's going to be mad about it."

Mom looked at the stock. "Well, don't worry," she said. "We'll talk to Dad. I don't think he'll be mad."

Mom went about skinning and cleaning the birds. Soon she called me over. "Say, these birds have all been shot through the neck. That's awfully good shooting, isn't it?"

"Yeah," I replied, "it's good shooting all right." Even that positive knowledge didn't lighten my heavy heart.

In about half an hour, Dad came home. Mom went to him right away and told him about my hunt. "Lee ran into a flock of spruce hens on the way home from school. I let him take the .22 and he shot three. Look," she said, holding up the pan of birds.

"Well," said Dad, "that's good hunting."

They were beautiful—their markings were striking and bold, yet they blended perfectly with the surrounding grass and bushes.

"That's only part of it," Mom said, "find the bullet holes."

Dad looked over the small carcasses. "Why, these are all shot through the neck!" he said in amazement. "Son, that's some shooting! I couldn't do better myself."

"I missed a lot of times, though," I mumbled.

"Who cares?" he exclaimed. "The neck of a spruce grouse is hardly any larger than a pencil. That's shooting!"

"Well, Dad, there's something I have to tell you," I began sadly as I handed him the rifle. "I cracked the stock of your rifle. I'm real sorry about it." I couldn't keep the tears back as I stood there before him.

"Let's have a look at it," Dad said gently as he took the rifle in his big hands. He flipped it over, wiggled it a bit, and said, "Y'know, I've got some high-powered furniture glue, real good stuff. Tomorrow we'll work on this and see what we can do."

"You mean you're not mad?" I asked.

"Naw," he smiled. "These foreign-made rifles are so flimsy they don't stand up to anything. I snapped one clean off, once. But tell me about your hunt," he went on. "That was a great piece of shooting, but you must have done some mighty careful stalking, too."

It turned out to be a great day after all. Mom roasted the grouse for supper. I said it was the best I'd ever tasted. Dad agreed. "When a man shoots his game properly and doesn't damage any meat," he said, "it's the best."

The next day, Dad glued and clamped the rifle stock. A few days later he brought it in from the shop. "Take a look at this," he said, handing me the repaired .22.

"Wow!" I exclaimed. "You fixed 'er real good. I can hardly even see the crack."

"She's as good as new," he agreed. "You know, I've been teaching you how to shoot and about handling guns safely for quite a while," he continued. "You've always paid attention and you've learned everything well. You're young but you're showing yourself to be responsible. From now on, this is your rifle. I'm giving it to you."

"It's going to be mine? My very own?" I asked.

"Yes," he replied, "it's yours."

"Oh, thanks Dad! Thanks a lot!" I cried with joy. "I promise

I'll take care of it. And I'll keep all the safety rules you taught me, too. And I ain't going to break the stock again, either."

Dad laughed. "Where do you want to hang your rifle, Son?" he asked.

"I want to hang it right up there under your .303," I replied. "Don't you think we should keep our hunting rifles together?"

"You bet we should!" he responded. "I'm going to drive a couple of nails in so we can do that right now!"

It's a Wolf!

ONCE IN A WHILE, WE HEAR OF WOLVES behaving in a way that is strangely and unexplainably out of character. I experienced this phenomenon the summer I was seven and my sister, Jean, was nine.

Timber wolves are different from any other animal. They are not cowardly or fear-driven, yet they almost always remain invisible in the bush. Some men who have lived long lives in the north say they could count on the fingers of one hand the times they have sighted wolves in the bush.

That summer, Dad hired Elwood, a northern Cree who was raised in the bush and knew the wilderness well, to cut some heavy brush north of the access road into our farmyard, about a hundred yards east of the house. Elwood was a big man, an even-tempered giant, soft-spoken and full of fun.

The brush was all cut and piled that day. The evening was cool and calm—an ideal time to burn the brush piles. Jean and I went out with Elwood after supper to watch the fire. I was barefoot and shirtless and soon realized I had underestimated the coolness of the evening. "I gotta get a shirt," I said to Elwood.

"Sure," the big man laughed. "I'll just light the pile by the road and wait till you get back to light the rest."

I raced to the house, put on my shirt, and started back down the road. In the meantime, Elwood touched off the first pile of brush. The fire took hold readily and, in minutes, a hearty blaze crackled.

Jean stood on the road twenty feet away. She was so absorbed in watching the fire she didn't notice the large dark form trotting silently toward her.

20

Both Elwood and Jean saw the wolf at the same moment.

"What is it?" Jean stammered.

"It's a wolf!" the big Cree shouted. He grabbed his axe and leaped between the frightened girl and the fearsome intruder.

Seemingly unperturbed, the wolf wheeled and loped back out the access road. He headed toward the river, south on the grid road.

"Run to the house, Jean!" Elwood hollered over his shoulder as he charged after the retreating wolf.

Jean needed no encouragement; cold fear swept through her. Terrified, she broke for the house running full out.

"It's a wolf!" she screamed at me as she streaked past.

I stopped, confused. I glanced from the sprinting Jean to the burly man, now also running for the house. Elwood was by no means graceful, but he could run. His big work boots pounded the packed dirt of the road. "Get back to the house!" he bellowed as he thundered past.

I had no idea what was happening, but it sounded serious. At top speed, I scampered for the house.

I reached the house to hear a distraught Elwood telling Dad, "I'm scared for Frances and the kids. Get the rifle! Get the truck! Hurry!"

Dad bounded into the house and came out immediately with his .303 and a box of shells. He tossed the rifle to Elwood who ripped the action open and began stuffing cartridges into the magazine. Dad ran for the garage. In seconds the old half-ton sputtered to life and then roared up to the front of the house.

"I'll ride in the back," Elwood shouted. He vaulted into the truck box and shoved extra shells into his pants pocket. The truck tore out of the yard faster than I'd ever seen it move. They headed south on the grid road.

"What's wrong, Jean? What happened?" I asked.

"It's a wolf! It's a wolf!" she repeated, trembling and frightened.

Finally Mom pieced the whole story together for me. While Elwood had worked for Dad all day, Elwood's wife, Frances, and their four children had spent the day at Hunter's farm, about a mile and a half south across the river. They were to walk back to our place that evening. The wolf Elwood had driven away had headed south on the same road Elwood's family would be travelling. He feared they would encounter the animal.

In less than ten minutes, the shooting started. I counted six shots. "He emptied the rifle," I said. We waited; it seemed like hours. He should have let Dad do the shooting, I thought. Then I remembered Dad saying, "That big Indian really knows the bush. He's a crack shot, too."

In about half an hour, we saw the truck returning from the south. Now, the three adults were squeezed into the cab, and the kids rode in the back.

I was really excited. "What happened, Dad? Did you get 'im?" I asked.

"We overtook the wolf at the top of Old Sam's hill," Dad replied. "Elwood hit him twice. He's badly wounded, but he made it over the bank and down into the thickets by the river. It's too dark now to go down there and track a wounded wolf. We continued south and met Frances and the family just across the bridge."

There was a lot of excited talk that evening as the two families rehashed the events and speculated about what could have happened.

"I'm scared," Jean said. "I'm scared to go out into the bush to pick berries. What if a wolf comes? I'm scared to walk to school. Maybe the wolf will come back."

"No, no," Elwood replied quietly. "That wolf is certainly dead by now. You don't need to be afraid. That animal must have been sick; wolves just don't behave that way."

"That's right," Dad agreed. "I've never heard of anything like this before, either. As Elwood said, the animal was probably sick. Besides, wolves almost always stay farther north. They can't adjust to the settled areas like the coyotes do."

Dad lit the Aladdin lamp. In no time Mom had the coffee pot on, and she brought up a sealer of strawberries from the cellar. The cheery light and friendly conversation began to calm our fears of lurking predators. Even Jean eventually overcame her fear of the bush and the peril of wolves.

I was sort of disappointed, though. I didn't get to go with Dad and Elwood, and heck, I sure wish I'd had a chance to see that wolf.

Once in a while, we hear of wolves behaving in a way that is strangely and unexplainably out of character.

Grandma Takes Charge

ON THE WAY HOME FROM SCHOOL one spring afternoon, I stopped at the rambling old farmhouse where my grandma lived with my Uncle Jake and my Aunt Lena. I could see right away that Grandma was concerned about something.

"Jacob is trying to get a pig back into the pen," she said, "and I think he needs some help."

I ran back to the barnyard. There was Bertha, the big sow, trotting warily across the yard. Uncle Jake and Toby, Grandma's dog, were trying to herd the sow back to her pen. I joined in, and for about half an hour we tried unsuccessfully to steer Bertha in the right direction. Suddenly, she veered around Uncle Jake. I jumped in front of her to head her off, but she just rumbled straight ahead and bowled me over like a ten-pin.

Uncle Jake rushed over. "Are you all right?" he asked, helping me to my feet.

"Yeah, I'm okay," I assured him. "Wow! She's like a runaway freight train, ain't she?"

"Ain't she though?" said Uncle Jake. "Bone-headed as they come, too!"

He got his lasso from the shed and began moving toward the sow. Bertha trotted away defiantly. My uncle shook out a loop and whirled the lasso over his head. Once, twice, swish! The rope snaked out and settled over Bertha's big head. She stepped through with one front leg and Uncle Jake snapped the rope taut.

"We got her now!" I hollered. Well, we had Bertha all right, but it looked more like she had us. She was dragging Uncle Jake across the barnyard, his boot heels plowing deep furrows in the soggy earth. I grabbed the tail end of the rope, and she dragged both of us.

Toby was in a frenzy of excitement. He darted forward and seized the big hog's curly tail. That tail stretched out as straight as a stick, about a foot-and-a-half long.

The adventure had become a circus. Bertha was squealing at ear-splitting decibels. Toby was hauling back on the sow's tail and growling ferociously. Uncle Jake was bellowing at the top of his voice. He had his feet planted and was trying to bring the huge porker to a standstill. When the bizarre humour of the scene struck me, I started to laugh. I laughed so hard that tears came. Just about then, Bertha's churning feet finally hit solid ground, and she bolted forward like a giant cannonball. I dropped the rope. Uncle Jake lost his footing but was determined to hang on. It seems that a two hundred-pound man on poor footing is no match for a four hundred-pound hog in high gear. In an instant, poor Uncle Jake was airborne. He landed on all fours, smack in the middle of a large puddle of barnyard muck!

My uncle was not a short-tempered man, but even patient folks have their limits. There on his hands and knees in that stinking mass, I guess Uncle Jake just lost control. His face turned as red as his mackinaw shirt and he bellowed in anger and frustration. He cussed that stubborn old sow and all her ancestors with an amazing thoroughness.

Just then, as though the whole comedy had been carefully scripted, who should appear but Grandma.

Uncle Jake got slowly to his feet, went to the watering trough and began washing his hands. Bertha stood nearby, panting from her rebellious overexertion. Her tail had curled up again. (I was afraid it never would!)

Grandma talked to Uncle Jake in German. I could hear the soft guttural tones but I understood nothing. I could tell she wasn't scolding, though. My uncle looked down and nodded, then muttered something in his mother's language.

Now Grandma turned her attention to the errant hog. She spoke softly to the animal in German. Bertha grunted rhythmically but didn't run off as she previously had when Uncle Jake and I came near.

Uncle Jake dried his hands on his shirt and rolled a cigarette from "the makin's" he carried in a pouch in his shirt pocket.

Grandma was taking charge and we stood silently by, watching and wondering what she would do.

Grandma shuffled over to the feed shed and pulled down an oat sheaf. Timothy and clover were mixed with the oats, and it had the fragrance of new-mown hay. The quiet little woman took up half the sheaf, walked over to the now placid sow, and jabbed it in her face.

In one aromatic moment, Bertha forgot all about freedom, rebellion, and making fools of a man, a boy, and a dog. Her tiny pig brain was instantly refocused on the love of her life—food. Just as the hog was about to open her mouth and reach for the tantalizing sheaf, Grandma snatched it away, said something in German, and began to walk toward the pigpen. Bertha lumbered after her like an obedient dog, grunting in either disappointment or anticipation, or perhaps both. Several times Grandma stopped to extend the sweet-smelling sheaf, only to snatch it away and walk on. In a few minutes, the two stood before the open pen door. Grandma held the sheaf out, longer this time. The hog's drooling mouth opened eagerly. At the last moment, the tempting morsel was withdrawn as before. Grandma said something in German and tossed the sheaf far into the pen.

Without hesitation, Bertha charged in, scooped up the sheaf, and began munching with obvious and unrestrained gusto.

Unhurriedly, Grandma closed the pen door and secured the latch.

Man, boy, and dog watched in silence. With gentleness and common sense, Grandma had accomplished in five minutes what we had failed to do in more than half an hour of noise, sweat, and all-out effort. We had nothing to say.

Grandma spoke kindly to her son. She smiled a lot. He grinned sheepishly, shrugged, and nodded a few times. Then she spoke in English, "You men must be tired and hungry. I'll go in and put the coffee pot on. And say," she said, "I've just taken a pan of cinnamon buns out of the oven, but I have my doubts about them. I may have put in too much brown sugar."

"Grandma," I replied, "there's no such thing as too much brown sugar!"

She laughed and started for the house. Uncle Jake and I followed.

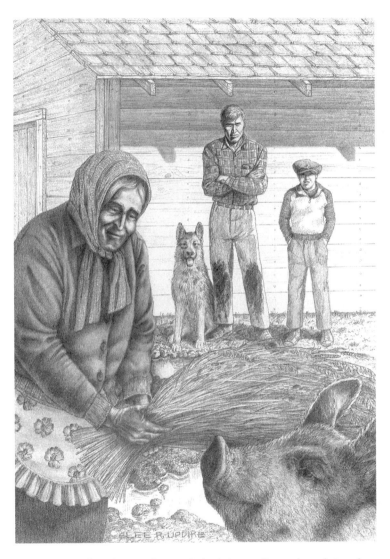

Grandma was taking charge and we stood silently by, watching and wondering what she would do.

As I thought about what happened that afternoon, I marvelled at Grandma's wisdom. Why, that cantankerous old Bertha had followed her right back into the pen for half an oat sheaf. And then, here we were following Grandma just as obediently.

"Uncle Jake," I said finally, "it's Grandma who's really in charge around here, isn't it?"

Uncle Jake looked at me sharply for a moment, then he grinned and replied, "You could be right."

"Good thing she is," I observed.

He laughed heartily. "C'mon," he said, "let's try them cinnamon buns."

The Forest Fire

THERE WASN'T A CLOUD IN THE SKY THAT SATURDAY. But then, there hadn't been a cloud in the sky on Friday either, or Thursday, Wednesday, or the week before, or the week before that. For the last month and a half there had been almost no rainfall. That's how it can get during a Saskatchewan dry spell.

A rickety old buggy creaked into our yard on the road from the south. It was Old Bill Judd. He reined up the team and chatted with Dad.

"By damn she's dry!" Old Bill observed. "Crops ain't gonna be worth nothing if we don't get a whole lotta rain mighty damn quick." The old farmer spat a wicked stream of tobacco juice onto the powdery dust of the road.

"Yeah, it's plenty dry all right," Dad agreed. "I heard on the radio it's raining hard in Alberta and moving east, though. Who knows, by morning we might be getting soaked ourselves."

"Guess I'll get on home," Old Bill chuckled. "Wouldn't wanta get caught in the downpour, now would I?" He spat, clucked to his horses, and left the yard at a trot.

It was early afternoon when we first noticed it: a plume of black smoke billowing skyward. I could tell by the expression on Dad's face—this was serious!

A moderate breeze from the south drove the rising black column northward. It increased in volume and intensity before our eyes. The cloud looked ominous and strangely out of place against the clear summer sky.

We found out later that Clarence, a young man cutting and piling brush on our neighbour Charlie's farm, had unwisely set fire to one of his piles. As wind-borne sparks ignited dry grass in half a dozen places, the fire swept quickly northward. Clarence

29

tried hopelessly and desperately to stomp out his mistake, but the flames leaped swiftly into the tinder-dry pine forest.

Dad threw an axe and a couple of shovels into the back of the old Chev half-ton. In minutes we were bouncing across the field toward Charlie's place.

I was nine that summer and had never seen a forest fire. Nothing quite prepares a person for that traumatizing experience.

The fire was an angry, orange and red monster devouring every living thing before it. The blinding, choking, stinging smoke, searing heat, and crackling roar of voracious flames was inescapable.

Most of the forest was Jack pine, with a sprinkling of large spruce, and a few groves of poplar. Jack pine is a tough, knotty wood. In the heat of summer, these trees are saturated with an extremely flammable resinous sap.

I watched, transfixed, as a giant pine, barely touched by fire in the lower branches, exploded into a ball of fire, shooting writhing flames thirty or forty feet straight up. The fierce heat created a savage updraft that sucked fire and flaming debris skyward.

Magnificent pine that had survived northern storms for a hundred years or more were destroyed in a matter of minutes. In my stricken mind, the forest fire was a force that could never be stopped. It was too big, too savage, too horrible. I wanted to turn and run.

Dad moved quickly to assess the size and direction of the fire. He determined that it was cutting a swath about a quarter of a mile wide and heading straight north, under the influence of a light south wind. The blaze wasn't moving much toward the east or west.

We jumped in the truck and headed home.

Our yard was full of vehicles. As people readied equipment, two rangers were outlining strategy to other men who had come to help. In short order a small convoy of vehicles streamed out the bush trail to the north and west, a small army setting out to engage in a battle I didn't think they could possibly win.

As the afternoon wore on, the insatiable flames surged relentlessly north, taking everything in their path. The eastern

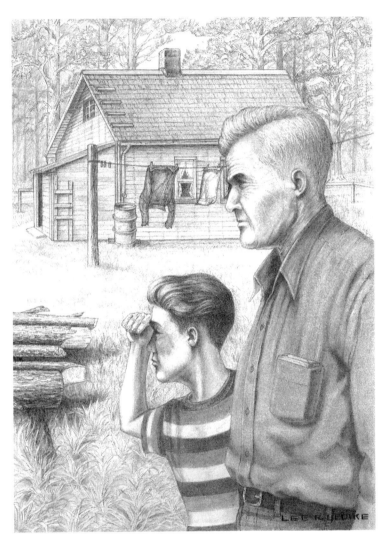

It was early afternoon when we first noticed it: a plume of black smoke billowing skyward.

edge of the fire ran parallel to the western boundary of our farm, with only a few hundred yards in between.

Fighting the fire head-on was hopeless. However, the cool of the evening was coming in a few hours. The plan was to make an all-out stand at the grid road farther north. The men hoped to bring the blaze under control by stopping it from crossing the treeless road allowance. However, late in the afternoon the wind increased and suddenly changed direction. It began to blow eastward and to drive the raging flames straight for our farm!

The southeast half of Dad's homestead was under cultivation—the rest was virgin timber. Now, with a stronger wind and a new direction, the fire moved on a broader front and attacked the pristine growth with renewed ferocity.

I was heartbroken and terrified at the same time. This was our land. I knew these trees. It was my hunting territory. I knew where every squirrel den was. I knew where the deer came to feed. I knew where the rabbits hid in the daytime. That spring, I had discovered a partridge nest under a willow bush. Young birds, twelve of them, followed their mother out of that nest. They were out there somewhere, trying to hide in the dry grass.

I watched the fire bear down on a familiar squirrel den under a huge Jack pine. Countless generations of the little animals had fattened themselves on pine seeds, sitting on the lower branches of that tree. Over the years, as they chewed open the seed-laden cones, fragments fell to form a broad mound about two feet deep around the base of the tree. Multiple den entrances penetrated the mound. As the flames swept near, the squirrels' instincts led them to the safest place they knew—the den. In less than a minute, they were cremated—every one of them.

At first I had been terrified of the fire; now I fiercely hated it, and I fought it with everything I had. I beat out ground fire with the back of my shovel. I shovelled dirt on flames and embers. I worked side by side with men I didn't even know. They too seemed to hate the fire and were doing everything they could to stop the flames.

I paused for a breather and looked around. I was immediately seized by a new fear. The inferno was not only destroying our trees—it was heading straight for the house and farm buildings.

I heard Dad and one of the rangers talking. "We'll do everything we can to save the buildings," George said, "but it's going to be touch and go. If it hits those trees by the barn, the barn's a goner. My biggest fear is that it will sweep around the corral and ignite the bluff that shelters the house."

"The wind is dropping," said Dad, "and with the cool of nightfall maybe we can get it stopped before it reaches the barn. But if it gets close, I want a tank of water at the north side of the house and some men to keep soaking the roof."

"You've got my word on it," the ranger replied. Grim-faced, the two men turned back to the fight.

Just after dusk, the wind ceased, and the air became cool and damp. Then, as though somewhere a great switch had been turned off, the fury of the blaze abated, and it became a creeping ground fire moving slowly and uncertainly through grass and brush. The fire line was now a stone's throw from our barn.

Suddenly there was a brilliant flash of light. A random spark had landed on the straw stack. In a moment, flames raced over the surface of a giant pile of wheat straw. The blaze was awesome.

Men appeared quickly out of the semi-darkness, turning their attention from the ground fire. The new fear was that sparks from the burning straw would set fire to the barn and the attached feed shed. Thankfully, our fears proved groundless. Airborne sparks from the light straw extinguished long before they settled to the ground.

In a short time, Mom and several women helping her appeared in the firelight. They brought coffee and a large basket of sandwiches. For the first time that day, all the men sat down, relaxed, and had lunch together. We sat or sprawled in the light of the burning stack. I looked at the dog-tired faces of those special men. Every face was blackened with smoke and soot, and streaked with sweat. I'm certain we could all have stretched out there on the parched grass and slept for hours.

After a time of rest, George spoke up. "Men," he said, "you've done one heck of a job! The worst is over and we've almost got 'er licked. Now, what we've got to do is make sure this ground fire is extinguished. The last thing we want is to have it flare up and take off again in the morning."

The men refilled their pack-pumps, grabbed their shovels, and finished the job. Some left earlier, but Dad and I patrolled the fire line until well past midnight. We had to be completely certain that the fire was out.

The next morning, Dad and I went out to survey the damage. In daylight, the devastation was obvious and horrific. It looked like a war had been fought on our land, and I guess that one had. Blackened snags marked spots where beautiful trees had stood. Grey ash covered the ground like an ugly blanket. In some places, the earth itself was scorched and blackened.

"It's terrible, Dad," I cried. "Everything is burned! Everything is dead! The squirrels are dead. The rabbits are dead. The birds are dead. It's like they never were."

"Yes," Dad replied. "Forest fires take a terrible toll."

"I hate forest fires!" I burst out. "Why did Ol' Clarence have to start that fire anyway? Why did he have to be so dumb?"

"Well, Clarence made a foolish mistake all right," Dad said. "He just didn't realize the danger."

"Yeah, but I'm just a kid," I said, "and even I know better than to light a fire when it's this dry."

"You've lived in this bush all your life, Son," Dad replied. "You understand these things. Clarence doesn't."

"Everything's still dead though, Dad," I said.

I felt heavy hearted and wondered if it was just a "kid thing." Maybe when I'm grown up, I thought, I'll be tougher and it won't matter that the animals and birds are dead, and that so many of our trees are burned up.

Dad didn't seem to be as sad as I was that morning. In fact, he was kind of optimistic. I didn't understand it.

"We've lost some trees and a lot of animals and birds have died," he said, "and it's right to be sad about that. But, we must also be thankful for what didn't happen and what we still have. We all fought as hard as we could, but it was more than our hard work that stopped the fire.

"What would have happened if the fire had come near the barn half an hour earlier?" he asked. "Or if the wind had not stopped when it did? We would have lost all our buildings and the rest of our trees. And right now, that fire would be destroying everything in the Fern Creek Valley. A forest fire in that heavy timber across the creek could burn for weeks. Maybe all the way up to the Torch River. Think about all the destruction and loss of wildlife that would cause. It's right to be sad about the damage and loss, but we must be thankful for what was saved."

"I guess I just couldn't see anything good about it at all," I replied.

"See that bluff of fire-killed pine?" he asked. "By next summer they'll be dry as a bone and dandy firewood. No doubt keep us in fuel for years. And look at that whole area," he continued, sweeping his arm north and west. "We can get a bulldozer in to clear the stumps and burned trees and then break up the land. I'll bet there's forty acres there, at least, good farmland, too."

"I see it now, Dad," I said. "What happened was bad, but some good can come out of it. What could have happened though is a hundred times worse."

He nodded and grinned. "We best head back and have some breakfast," he said. "You hungry?"

"You bet," I replied, "I'm starved!"

A Problem with Peaches

NOTHING SEEMED TO FIT RODDY MCKAY. Maybe that's the way it is when you're a grown man and barely five feet tall. His pants, a couple of sizes too large, draped loosely over his spindly legs. The brown windbreaker he wore looked like it was hanging on a scarecrow. His horn-rimmed glasses perched on a generous beaklike nose, magnifying his eyes.

The most arresting feature of Roddy McKay, however, had nothing to do with his appearance. It was his voice. The pint-sized man possessed a deep, resonant, giant lumberjack kind of voice that produced many a smile when folks realized its source.

It was a good five-mile walk from our farm to the village of White Fox. My friend Reggie and I hiked in one Saturday afternoon for the matinee. Roy Rogers was playing at the Roxy. We each had the fifteen cents admission and a few cents over. We figured if we pooled our finances we could split a pack of gum. We stopped at the Co-op Grocery to make our purchase. It was there that we encountered little Roddy McKay and his big crate of peaches.

"You look like a couple of strong boys," the big voice rumbled. "Would you mind carrying this case of peaches over to my house for me? It's not too far."

"Sure, we're the guys who can do it, Mr. McKay," my friend Reggie said. "Our price is a dime apiece."

"Oh, I couldn't pay you for it," the small man replied.

"Well how about giving us each a peach, then?" Reggie asked.

"Okay, okay," the big voice conceded. "You can each have a peach."

"You got yourself a deal!" Reggie exclaimed. "We'll get 'er over to your place in no time flat."

Reggie was a year and a half older than me. Even at ten, he had an engaging smile, an appealing personality, and a growing entrepreneurial spirit. I didn't seem to possess any of those qualities, so Reggie was usually our spokesman.

My talkative friend and I soon discovered that the crate of fruit was extremely heavy. We each took an end and followed the slight figure out the door. After a block and a half, Reg asked, "Where's your place, Mr. McKay?"

"Just a few more blocks," came the reply.

The little man finally pointed out a tiny Insulbrick-sided house on the corner. He fumbled a long time with the lock until at last the door swung open and we manoeuvred the crate into the kitchen and hoisted it onto the table.

"The job's done, Mr. McKay," puffed Reggie. "Whack open that crate and give us our peaches."

"Well, uh, the Missus isn't here," he replied. "I don't think I should open it." There was a strange whine in the big voice.

"Listen, that crate's heavy," Reggie said, "an' you promised."

"All right, all right," Roddy replied nervously. He pried the wooden top off the crate with a claw hammer, and we each selected a peach. We turned to leave when the door latch rattled and heavy steps sounded in the hall.

Reg and I both took a step back when "the Missus" stomped in. Mrs. McKay was a huge woman who towered over little Roddy. Big boned and grossly overweight, I guessed she would tip the scale at 250 pounds, easily.

The big lady scowled. "Got the peaches home I see," she said. Then she noticed the crate was open. "Why did you open the crate?" she growled at her husband.

Mrs. McKay shifted her attention to Reg and me, noticing that we each had a peach. "Who are these boys and why do they have peaches?" Her coarse voice was harsh and accusing.

"Well, my dear," Roddy's big voice quavered, "these boys carried the crate home for us and I gave them each a peach ..."

"What?" the Missus thundered. "You gave away my peaches? You boys put those peaches back, right now!"

"Nope!" Reggie retorted. "We earned 'em. We agreed to carry the crate over from the Co-op for a peach each. Mr. McKay promised."

"I'm getting outta here," I mumbled and started for the door, clutching my peach firmly. Reggie was at my heels.

"You put them peaches back, you peach-thieving brats!" Roddy's Missus roared. We stampeded out the door and didn't look back. As we scampered away we could hear the huge woman railing at her diminutive husband for more than a block.

"What an old hag!" Reggie said.

"Yeah," I agreed, "and she's twice the size of Roddy. If she ever whacks him, he's a goner."

"Man," observed Reg, "I think he's a goner already, living with a mean old crab like her.

"Hey, I'm hungry," he said. "Let's eat our peaches."

It didn't take long to discover that my peach was not very tasty, not very tasty at all.

Reggie took a big bite, then he spat on the sidewalk. "Pah!" he exploded. "This peach is green or something. It tastes terrible!" He reared back and fired the unappetizing fruit at a lamppost. The impact made a satisfying splat. "If that don't beat all!" he said. "That crate weighed a ton; we lugged it for six blocks over to Roddy's place; we got yelled at by old two-ton herself; and now the peaches are no good. It just don't pay to help folks."

"Well, we did a good deed anyway," I said.

"Yeah, yeah, and who cares?" he grumbled.

"Say," I said, "we better get over to the theatre. It could be three o'clock by now!"

"You're right!" Reg exclaimed. "We could be missing the cartoon right now!"

I started to laugh. "I think we already saw the cartoon."

"Haw! Haw!" Reggie laughed. "Roddy and the Missus, what a pair! Ain't they right outta the comics?"

We sprinted for the Roxy and made it with five minutes to spare. The cartoons were good. Roy Rogers was good. We soon forgot about our problem with the peaches.

On the long walk home we had lots of time to talk. "Hey Reg," I said, "I guess you're hopin' your mom gets a nice crate of peaches when she goes to town next week."

"Like heck!" he snorted. "From now on I'm sticking to blueberries."

The little man finally pointed out a tiny Insulbrick-sided house on the corner.

Jersey Black Giant

ONE SPRING, MOM STRUCK A DEAL with a distant relative and came away with a new rooster. No one in the whole district had ever seen a bird like this one. He was jet black and absolutely enormous. His body was larger and heavier than the average turkey. He was of a breed called Jersey Black Giant. Everyone agreed that the name fit the rooster. Mom was very proud of the giant and liked to show him off when folks stopped by.

I was nine that year. I was never very concerned with chickens, but this one was different. I had never seen anything so big with feathers in my life.

At first I admired the big black addition to the farm, but my admiration soon turned to disgust. The giant proved to be so ill-tempered and aggressive that I came to dislike him, and I always gave him a wide berth on the farmyard.

One Saturday afternoon I was working on a project that required whittling a three-foot poplar stick to a smooth surface. Being thoroughly engrossed in the task, I didn't notice Mom's rooster getting ready to tackle me from the blind side. Just in the nick of time, I heard his heavy footsteps and jumped out of harm's way.

Thinking the rooster had calmed down, I tried to ignore him. This was clearly a mistake because, a second later, he charged again. His giant breast hit the back of my legs like a pile-driver. I was flattened—by a chicken—in a most undignified manner.

Incensed, I leaped to my feet and kicked the black giant. That was another mistake. His huge body was so solid it felt like I had kicked a big old Jack pine. Certain I had broken my ankle, I fell to the ground clutching it in pain.

The Jersey Black Giant wasn't through yet. This time he flew at me and pummelled me with his wings. He raked my back with his sharp spurs and pecked me three or four times with his black giant beak.

By this time I was really hurting and really mad. "I ain't getting beat up by no chicken!" I yelled. I grabbed the poplar stick I had been working on and rifled it at the big rooster. The stick made an ominous whirring sound. It rotated like the blades of a miniature helicopter as it sped toward its target. It struck the big bird on the back of the head, and he instantly toppled forward, his wings and legs convulsing.

"Good grief!" I groaned. "I killed Mom's prize rooster." I rushed to the fallen giant.

I glanced around. There, to my dismay, was Dad. Obviously he had witnessed the whole thing. He began to hurry over and my fears increased with each of his strides. Then I noticed that the rooster seemed to be reviving. I felt a cautious relief. Perhaps things were not as bad as they had seemed.

Dad paid no attention. He seized the big rooster by the legs and hustled him over to the woodpile. After one swift stroke of the axe, Mom's Jersey Black Giant was flopping headless on the grass.

At that moment, Mom burst out the front door. "What have you done to my rooster?" she yelled. "What have you done to my rooster?"

I don't mind saying that I sure wished I were someplace else just then. I was plenty scared and more than a little confused.

"Well," Dad drawled, "your rooster sort of had an accident. I figured the best thing to do was to put him out of his misery as soon as possible."

"Is that so?" Mom bristled. "I'd like to hear about this accident."

"Yeah, well," said Dad, "why don't we have some coffee and I'll tell you all about it." With that, my parents went into the house.

Still rooted to the spot, I wondered if I had missed something. I expected big trouble ahead with Mom and probably Dad too. Yet, they were having coffee and here I was outside. It didn't make sense.

I waited a while and finally, with some trepidation, entered the house. Mom and Dad sat at the kitchen table, chatting amiably.

Dad motioned me to come near. He lifted the back of my shirt and showed Mom the welts left by the giant's spurs.

"My word!" she exclaimed. "If I'd known he was that mean I'd have taken him to the chopping block myself."

"I'm sorry for killing your rooster, Mom," I mumbled. "It's just that he wouldn't back off an'..."

"You didn't kill him, Son," Dad interrupted with a chuckle. "You just stunned him. He had it coming, too. I've had a couple of run-ins with that bird myself. I nearly took the pitchfork to him last week. We just can't put up with that kind of behaviour from any chicken, regardless of his pedigree. Mom feels the same way."

"I sure do," Mom agreed. "And the Jersey Black Giant is going to be guest of honour at Sunday dinner. We're going to Grandma's right now to invite her and the family to come over tomorrow."

"Oh boy," I said. I was feeling much relieved, indeed.

What a special Sunday dinner it was, like Christmas and Thanksgiving all rolled into one. Mom prepared a tremendous meal in spite of the difficulty she had fitting the giant into her largest roasting pan.

"I'm sure sorry to hear about the accident that happened here yesterday," my Uncle Jake said in mock sympathy.

"I'm not!" I exclaimed.

"I'm not sorry either," Mom said.

"Say, Mary," Uncle Frank said, "I recollect you did a lot of braggin' about this big rooster of yours. Maybe he wasn't so great after all, huh?"

"He was the biggest rooster I'd ever seen," said Mom. "I was real proud of him. I still am; he's the nicest bird I ever roasted." Mom passed the loaded platter to her younger brother. "Here Frank," she said. "Do a little less talking and eat the biggest drumstick you've ever had."

"I'm sure sorry to hear about the accident that happened here yesterday," my Uncle Jake said in mock sympathy.

Me 'n' Uncle Jake

THERE WAS NOBODY LIKE MY UNCLE JAKE. He always had time for me and he listened and didn't laugh when I said dumb stuff. I could tell that Uncle Jake really cared about me because he didn't treat me like I was just a kid, even when other grown-ups were present.

I was excited when Uncle Jake drove his team into our farmyard one Saturday morning in January when I was ten. He was hauling a sleigh-box full of firewood for someone in the village of White Fox.

Uncle Jake asked if I would like to make the trip with him. "I sure need the company," he said. My mom consented, on the condition that I wear lots of warm clothes.

In short order, we were on the road. It was a nice day—for January in Saskatchewan. The temperature was fifteen below zero, but the sun was bright on the blanket of white that covered our world. The horses moved briskly, and the sleigh glided easily over the well-beaten track. Uncle Jake let me drive. It was a very good day.

The horses were hardly a well-matched team. Bess, the mare on the right, was a short-limbed, chunky bay. She was nervous and unfriendly. Old Prince, on the left, was my favourite horse of all time. He was a huge dark brown gelding. In his prime he had been a magnificent animal. "Best I ever seen," Uncle Jake had said. But now Prince was old and bony. His joints were stiff, and he had nowhere near his old strength and stamina.

A mile south of our farm, the winding White Fox River flowed north and east. The lazy stream seemed almost insignificant as it snaked its way between massive banks that had once cradled a mighty river. As we approached the river, Prince began acting strangely. He seemed nervous and wanted to break into a run. Uncle Jake took the lines and held him back.

"Boy, Ol' Prince is frisky this morning!" I laughed.

Uncle Jake smiled. "Prince is afraid of the hill," he said quietly. I didn't understand what he meant, but the big horse became even more agitated as we neared the hill.

The downgrade was very gradual, and we made the long descent without incident. Uncle Jake let the horses trot the last hundred yards. Prince tried awkwardly to gallop. I was really worried about what was happening to him, but I didn't let Uncle Jake know.

The hill on the south side was much steeper than the one on the north side. At the foot of the south hill, Uncle Jake reined up. "We'll give 'em a breather before we start up," he explained.

My uncle climbed down and walked around to Old Prince's head. He talked softly to the big horse and stroked him gently. Prince stopped trembling, but he was still extremely nervous.

Uncle Jake is right, I thought, Old Prince is scared of this hill, really scared. I wasn't sure why, but I was getting scared too.

At last my uncle climbed up into the seat. He took up the lines and clucked to the team. They hit the collars together; this time Uncle Jake didn't hold them back. We gathered speed and both horses began to run, but soon the steep incline and the weight of the load took their toll. Now I saw why Old Prince was afraid; he was afraid he couldn't make it up that hill one more time.

Suddenly Uncle Jake was standing, his feet wide spread. He gripped the lines in his left hand, and, with their long ends in his right hand, he began to whip Old Prince. The old gelding was frantic. His own panic added to the awkwardness of his stiffened tired limbs. He slipped; he stumbled; his huge hoofs gouged into the icy slope, groping desperately for the solid footing he just couldn't find. Uncle Jake shouted and flayed Prince's bony rump. "Come on Prince!" Crack! "Get up Prince!" Crack! Crack! Crack!

I was terrified. I couldn't believe what was happening. I cried.

The mare crouched low in the harness, seeming to find more leverage and better traction that way. Her heavily muscled thighs drove her forward with quick powerful strides.

Old Prince's breath was coming in great heaving gasps.

Then, in a split second, what I feared the most happened. Old Prince stumbled and fell heavily.

"Get up Prince! Get up!" Uncle Jake roared. Crack! Crack! "Come on Prince!" Crack! "Get up Boy! You can do it!" Crack! Crack!

With a groan, Old Prince somehow lurched to his feet and stumbled valiantly on. Sweat drenched his dark hide.

At last the nightmare was over. The hill was behind us and the sleigh creaked to a stop on level ground. We made it.

Bess had survived the ordeal in good shape. Though she was breathing hard, she was hardly sweating. However, I was certain Old Prince would never recover. His front feet were spread apart, his head hung down, and his sides heaved with every tortured breath.

As soon as we stopped, Uncle Jake reached under the seat and brought out a tattered grey horse blanket. He vaulted to the ground and gently covered the big horse's steaming frame. Then he went to Prince's head and began to pet him and talk to him softly. I heard him tell Prince he was the best horse he'd ever seen and that he was proud of him. I strained to hear more but could not. Old Prince pressed his forehead against Uncle Jake's big chest. They stood that way for a long time as Uncle Jake talked softly and gently stroked the aged horse.

As I shivered on the sleigh, I tried to understand. It seemed to me that Uncle Jake had badly mistreated Old Prince. Now though, I was sure I could see love and strength flowing from the big powerful man into the worn tired body of the old horse.

After some time, Prince stood erect again. He lifted his head high and shook it, as though shaking off the memory of the hill. He no longer trembled and his breathing was back to normal. Ol' Prince is going to be okay, I thought, somewhat cautiously.

Uncle Jake carefully folded the blanket back off Prince's neck then climbed up on the sleigh beside me.

I couldn't help it; I just had to let it all out. "Uncle Jake, how could you treat Ol' Prince like that?" I wailed. "I thought you loved Ol' Prince. I thought he was gonna die there on the hill." The words all tumbled out as tears stung my cold cheeks.

He talked softly to the big horse and stroked him gently. Prince stopped trembling, but he was still extremely nervous.

Uncle Jake's eyes were kind, and he remained silent until I had said it all. Then he spoke. "Me and Prince go back a long way, you know. I want to keep him as long as I can, but I can only afford to feed two horses. Besides, my stable is only large enough for a team. Prince seems to understand that if he can't handle the work, I can't keep him. Once, maybe twice, in a winter he may have a tough hill to climb. But he knows I'll help him all I can. Then, come spring, he has the whole back pasture all to himself. Me and Ol' Prince are kinda working together so we can stay together longer. Do you understand?" he asked.

"I ... I think so," I mumbled. I felt ashamed for crying in front of Uncle Jake. I had acted just like a kid. I wondered if he would treat me like one from then on.

Uncle Jake picked up the lines and spoke to the team. We moved off smoothly. Old Prince was himself again. We rode in silence for a while. The sun seemed warmer somehow, and I had stopped shivering.

"You know what, Uncle Jake?" I said finally. "I think you an' me both love Ol' Prince a whole lot."

Uncle Jake grinned. "You betcha!" he said as he handed me the lines. "You betcha!"

On Target—In Trouble

IT WAS A TWO-MILE WALK TO THE COUNTRY SCHOOL. My sister, Jean, and I often walked to and from school with my friend Reggie. One day we had only gone a quarter of a mile on the way home when Uncle Jake drove up beside us in his old McLaughlin-Buick.

"Want a ride?" he asked with a big grin.

"You bet!" we shouted and piled into the big sedan.

We had hardly gotten into high gear when suddenly the steady drone of the big six-cylinder motor became a deafening roar.

Uncle Jake looked kind of peeved as he braked to a stop. "Damn muffler," he muttered as he shoved the door open and jumped out. We all clambered out after him. The Buick barked out the blown muffler like an old tractor. Uncle Jake knelt down just ahead of the hind wheel on the passenger side. He wiggled his head and shoulders under the wide running board and surveyed the damage. My uncle's broad rump seemed to jut up in the air a long way, and his worn jeans were extremely tight.

Reggie—that incurable prankster—picked up a stone and pretended to chuck it at the inviting target.

"No! No! No!" Jean mouthed the words silently.

I nodded toward the big backside and dared Reggie to give it his best shot. I was sure that even Reggie wouldn't be foolhardy enough to accept the challenge.

To my amazement, he reared back and fired. A resounding smack assured us that the rock had landed right on target. Mind you, how could a guy miss such a generous target at a range of five or six feet?

We weren't prepared for the immediate consequences of that bull's eye. A thunderous bellow came from under the car, then a clunk, and a hearty stream of cuss words. Uncle Jake, startled by the missile that had hit his backside, had bumped his head on the car frame. The painful impact dislodged a shower of dried mud and dirt that rained down on the back of his neck.

He backed out from under the car, as cantankerous as an old bear breaking out of hibernation. He was red-faced and plenty riled as he pawed the dirt out of his hair and off his neck.

Jean and I were rooted to the spot, but at the first bellow, Reggie took off for the bluff across the road in the Collins's pasture. Reg was not an especially fast runner, but that day he was highly motivated. I'd never seen him run so fast.

Uncle Jake assessed the situation at a glance: my sister and I stood like open-mouthed statues; Reggie was in full flight. Instantly, Uncle Jake was in overdrive. His big size twelves pounded across the dirt road and through the grass of the road allowance. His running style wasn't pretty, but he covered the ground at an astonishing clip. Poor Reggie didn't have a chance. He jettisoned his lunch box, but it made no difference. Several yards before he reached the pasture fence, a bearlike arm scooped him off his feet.

Uncle Jake carried Reg back to the car. Once there, he set the scared ten-year-old back on his feet. "We best be going," he said. His face was expressionless.

Nervously, we got into the car. I sat in front. Everyone looked straight ahead. The noise level inside the car would have made conversation difficult, but it didn't really matter; no one said a word on the ten-minute drive to Uncle Jake's place. I stole a lot of side-glances at my uncle. Once I caught him struggling to conceal a grin. I relaxed and sat back in the overstuffed cushions of the Buick. In a few minutes, we turned into the driveway and Uncle Jake stopped to let us out.

"Bye! Thanks for the ride," we all chorused.

"You're welcome. See you soon, kids," he said, still deadpan.

"Reggie, you dummy!" Jean scolded. "Why did you do such a stupid thing?"

"I shouldn't have done it," Reg admitted, "but I just couldn't seem to help it. Besides, Lee dared me."

"Good grief," I exclaimed. "I didn't think you'd actually do it."

"Boy, was I scared!" Reggie confided. "I thought he was

My uncle's broad rump seemed to jut up in the air a long way, and his worn jeans were extremely tight.

gonna whup me good. I wish I hadn't chucked that stone. Your Uncle Jake is a real good guy, and now he's mad at me—prob'ly gonna get even, too."

"Naw," I replied. "Uncle Jake ain't like that; he don't hold grudges. Besides, he was trying to keep from laughing."

"Was he really?" he asked.

"Sure," I responded. "I saw him."

"He sure looked mad, and he didn't talk and laugh like he usually does," said Reg.

"Maybe it's just a warning," I suggested. "You know; you had your fun, you got away with it, don't pull anything else. Something like that."

"Well, I ain't pulling anything on him again, no sir!" Reg vowed. "He scared the heck outta me. I never thought a guy that big could move that fast."

"Just a suggestion, Reg," I said. "Maybe you should apologize for pingin' him in the rump."

"Well, I s'pose so," he replied, "but not right away, I'm too scared to bring the subject up."

"If you'd listened to me in the first place," Jean chided, "none of this would have happened."

"Aw heck, Jean," Reg retorted, "if we listened to you all the time we wouldn't have any fun at all."

"This was fun?" Jean snapped.

"Well, sorta ..." he said, "sorta funny." Then he snickered right out loud.

I could see it coming. Reggie started to giggle. Soon he was doubled over, shaking with laughter. I couldn't help it; I joined in and laughed as hard as he did.

"You guys are crazy!" my sister screeched. "You're just crazy!" But eventually, even Jean caught the humour of it all and had a good laugh too.

After we all calmed down, I said, "Look, this was kind of funny, all right, but we ain't pulling anything on Uncle Jake, ever again, right?"

"Right!" said Jean. "Uncle Jake is a very nice person and he deserves to be treated with respect."

"Yeah, you're right," Reggie agreed. "Besides, he runs just too darn fast."

Toby Learns a Lesson

FOR MY SISTER AND ME, STOPPING AT GRANDMA'S house was the highlight of our walk to and from school.

The summer I was eleven and Jean was thirteen, Mom and Grandma decided that Jean and I would pick up a gallon pail of milk to take home with us from Grandma's house each day after school. At the time, Uncle Jake and Grandma had cows but we didn't. This arrangement meant that we would drop off the empty pail each morning on the way to school, and pick up the full one on the way home.

We loved stopping at Grandma's. She was always cheerful and kind and often fixed us an after-school snack. Uncle Jake and Aunt Lena were fun, too. Sometimes Uncle Frank was there, which made our after-school visits even better.

However, there was one big problem with our daily visits to Grandma's—Toby. Toby was a good farm dog, I suppose, but Toby was mean, and Toby was big, really big. Toby bit my sister once, and he bit me quite a few times, although he never actually drew blood.

We told Grandma and Uncle Jake, but they just couldn't believe that Toby would be anything but playful. "He's just a big silly pup; he won't hurt you," they would say. Or, "He's just playing. Don't be afraid of him."

I talked to my Dad. "Aw, Toby is just a big dumb mutt," he said with a laugh. "Face up to him and he won't hurt you."

Well, I was facing up to Toby, twice a day, five days a week, and I was afraid of him. He bit me whenever he felt like it, but no one believed me or seemed to care that it was happening.

Every time we arrived at Grandma's house, Toby would

stand on the front step barking and growling. I would have to push past him to reach the door.

One morning, just as I reached up to knock on Grandma's door, Toby grabbed my left forearm in his big ugly mouth. I tried to pull free, but he just gripped tighter. His jaws felt like a steel vise. His eyes were pale, almost yellow, and full of contempt. He glared into my face and growled deep in his throat. I felt helpless and scared in his grasp.

"Grandma! Grandma!" Jean cried out.

As soon as Grandma opened the door the dog released my arm and began to wag his tail and behave in a friendly manner.

"Grandma, Toby grabbed my arm!" I exclaimed. "I tried to get loose but he wouldn't let go."

"Yes, he really did," Jean said excitedly, "and he was growling the whole time!"

"But look, he's happy to see you," said Grandma. "He really likes you. He's only playing."

Uncle Jake appeared in the doorway. "Yeah, he's just a big pup. Don't be scared of him; he won't hurt you," he said.

We continued on to school. I felt bad because Grandma's dog was so mean and sneaky, and no one would believe me when I tried to tell them. I felt even worse because I was so intimidated by the animal.

On the way home from school that day, Jean and I talked about Toby. "I hate to say it," I began, "but I'm starting to feel like I don't want to go to Grandma's anymore. I know it isn't right, but I'm starting to hate that dog."

"I don't like him either," said Jean, "and I'm just as scared of him as you are."

"The dog bites me and nobody will believe it," I muttered, "and there's nothing we can do about it." In frustration, I threw a stone at a post in the Collins's fenceline. As the stone cracked against the post, an idea began to form in my troubled mind. "Hey, maybe there is something we can do," I said.

"What?" my sister asked.

"Watch," I said and fired another stone. The rock pinged as it ricocheted off the weathered tamarack post. A shower of bark fragments fluttered to the ground.

Grandma's dog took off for the bush like a prairie jackrabbit, and he never looked back.

"You're going to throw a stone at Toby?" she asked incredulously.

"Stones," I corrected. "As many as it takes."

"But you can't do that!" she exclaimed, "Grandma and Uncle Jake would be offended."

"Why should they even know?" I shot back. "They don't come to the door until I knock, do they?"

"What if you miss?" she questioned.

"I won't miss. He's a big target and I'll get close," I replied. "That dog is mean and he's a bully," I continued, "just like the bullies at school. You gotta fight back. You can't let others bully you. Well, it's time to fight back, and Toby needs to learn a lesson."

"Maybe you're right," Jean replied, "but your plan still frightens me."

I carefully selected six egg-sized stones. I put three in my left jacket pocket and three in the right.

As we approached Grandma's, we could hear Toby barking. "This is the showdown," I said grimly. I was nervous, but determined to put my plan into action. I tried to be nonchalant as I walked to within twenty feet of the house. Toby occupied the front step, barking as usual. I gripped carefully, set, and fired the first stone as hard as I could. It was a perfect shot. It struck him in the centre of his broad chest.

The dog was startled and jolted backwards. Nervously he turned sideways. The second missile was already on its way. It made a meaty "smack!" as it cracked into his ribs. Toby gave a little yelp, sprang off the step, and began running uncertainly, looking over his shoulder.

I ran after him, winding up for number three. I put everything into it; the stone streaked toward its target. With more than a little luck, it struck the fleeing Toby at the base of his skull, behind his left ear. The impact stunned him momentarily; he stumbled, recovered, and running full out, disappeared into the bushes.

I strode confidently to the front door and knocked.

We had a very good visit, although I could see that Jean was worried about what would happen when we made our exit. I checked my right pocket occasionally, too, just to be sure the stones were still there.

When it was time to leave, I opened the door. Toby was in his place on the step. He leaped up the moment he saw me and darted around the corner of the house. I felt very good as we walked out of Grandma's yard that afternoon.

I stashed the remainder of my stones under a saskatoon bush out by the road.

The next morning, I re-armed myself with the stones before we entered the yard. Toby barked a little from the step then stood nervously watching our approach. When we were about twenty feet away, I suddenly thrust my hand into my jacket pocket—like a gunslinger reaching for his six-gun in the days of the old west. Grandma's dog took off for the bush like a prairie jackrabbit, and he never looked back.

"You can knock this time," I told my sister. "It's safe now."

That afternoon we again stopped at Grandma's. This time Toby didn't bark while he paced on the front step. As soon as we entered the yard he trotted quickly down the road to the barnyard and out of sight.

As we were leaving, Uncle Jake came to the door with us. Toby scampered around the corner of the house when he saw me. Uncle Jake came outside and we talked for a few minutes. "Funny thing about Toby," he said. "Every time you show up, he takes off."

"Yeah, funny thing," I said.

Uncle Jake's eyes searched my face for a moment. "See you tomorrow," he finally said.

In time I gave up carrying stones to Grandma's house. Heck, I didn't need them; Toby had given up on being a bully. Oh, he'd bark dutifully when we came, but he'd move aside when we went to the door. He never bit Jean or me again. Although I never told Grandma or Uncle Jake about the stones, I have a hunch Uncle Jake had it figured out. Still, he never mentioned anything.

Sometimes difficulties have a strange way of working out. In the process, we often learn a lesson, or help someone else learn one—even if that someone is Grandma's dog.

Saving Mopus

MY UNCLE FRANK OWNED PROPERTY adjacent to the Torch River, fifteen miles north of our farm. His land was rich with excellent spruce timber, so he built a little sawmill to harvest it. The mill was a result of my uncle's inventive genius—most folks were astonished that a man who had never seen the inside of a school classroom could design and build something so complicated and that it would actually work. Well, that mill worked very well indeed. "She works like a damn!" Uncle Frank said.

During the summer holidays the year I was twelve, my uncles asked if I would like a job working with them in the sawmill for three weeks. I jumped at the chance. It was always fun being with my two big uncles, mostly because they treated me like a grown-up. Heck, for three weeks I'd be a man, working in the mill and earning money besides.

Uncle Jake and I made the trip north with Buck and King, his new team, and a wagonload of supplies. Uncle Jake's dog, Mopus, accompanied us, of course. Mopus was short legged, overweight, and pint sized—a dumpy little mutt—but he had a huge ego. He swaggered around as though the whole trip was somehow for his benefit.

The days were long and the work was hard, but over the three weeks we sawed a whole lot of spruce lumber.

It seemed that all too soon it was time to load the wagon and head south. Buck and King were young and full of life, and we made good time on our trip.

Eight miles south of Uncle Frank's, we passed the Krugers' place. The Krugers had a large family, mostly boys. One of the Kruger boys used a dog team on his trapline, and in the summer he let the animals run loose.

As we drew near the trail into the Kruger's yard, five large dogs bounded out, barking furiously. They surrounded the wagon and followed us down the road, snarling and barking in a threatening manner.

I noticed that Mopus was doing some furious barking himself, his little hackles raised. It sounded like he was challenging the whole pack of dogs, eager to do battle.

Then, to my amazement and horror, Mopus waddled over to the edge of the wagon box and leaped over the side.

Perhaps he saw himself as a conquering hero, throwing himself to the ground to whip those dogs single-handedly. In reality, his jump carried him less than a foot and a half. He belly-flopped awkwardly onto the sun-baked road, only to have the steel-tired rear wheel of the wagon slam over his pudgy middle.

Uncle Jake's face went white. Muscles bulged under his faded grey shirt as he hauled the trotting team back on their haunches. "Whoa!" he bellowed. "Hold 'em!" he shouted, as he shoved the lines into my hands.

Empty-handed, Uncle Jake was over the side in a flash. He hit the road on a dead run, back to where five snarling sleigh dogs circled a motionless dark form.

I was terrified. Mopus looked dead and I was afraid Uncle Jake would be torn to shreds by the Kruger boys' dogs. I was also afraid that I wouldn't be able to hold the excited and prancing young team. I gripped the lines with all my strength. "I gotta hold 'em! I gotta hold 'em!" I kept saying to myself. I braced my feet against the front of the wagon box and sawed the lines back and forth, as I had seen Uncle Jake do at times. "Whoa!" I shouted, trying to make my voice sound deep like Uncle Jake's.

I tried to sit sideways so I could watch the horses and still see what was happening behind me on the road.

I saw my uncle charge around the back of the wagon. Five dogs advanced toward him as one. He didn't slacken his pace but ran into the midst of them and lashed out with a thunderous kick that sent the nearest animal sprawling. A huge black brute tried to retreat too late, and, with a whump, a size twelve work boot landed in his ribs. He slunk away. The pack was now disorganized and they withdrew slightly. Uncle Jake ignored them and went straight to Mopus.

Uncle Jake knelt down on the dirt road by the inert form of his little dog. Kruger's dogs circled the two of them and began advancing slowly, stiff-legged, hackles raised, snarling. Uncle Jake looked up, his sandy hair spilling over his forehead, and his blue eyes blazing with a fierce intensity. "Get back!" he roared. "Get back!" His voice crackled with authority. My uncle looked fearlessly into the eyes of each of those dogs. He literally stared them down, forcing them into submission with the authority of his gaze.

Tenderly, Uncle Jake picked Mopus up. The dogs backed off and let him pass. As he moved to the front of the wagon, the circle tightened again. Uncle Jake turned impatiently. The courage of the animals seemed to wilt under his withering glare, and they drew back again.

Cradling the little dog gently in one arm like a mother holding her baby, Uncle Jake swung aboard. As soon as he was seated, the whole pack of dogs leaped up at the wagon box, snarling and barking with renewed ferocity. I didn't understand it then, but when I recall the events of that day I wonder if even dogs sometimes try to "save face."

At a soft command from their master, the team sprang forward, immediately breaking into a gallop. I couldn't hold them any more. My uncle reached over, grabbed the lines with one big hand, and brought the horses under control in a moment. "Easy," he said, "easy." They settled down to a steady trot. The wagon rattled and bounced and we soon left the Krugers' dogs far behind.

Uncle Jake held Mopus for a long time while I drove.

"Is he going to be all right?" I asked finally.

"I don't know," he replied. "He's tough as nails though, I know that." Mopus whimpered softly as Uncle Jake explored his injured body with his kind hands.

We rode in silence again.

"That was a brave thing you did, Uncle Jake," I finally said.

He looked up quickly and seemed embarrassed. "Well," he said, "I don't have a lot of fear of animals."

"I was scared," I said.

"Hey, you did a great job of holding the horses," my uncle said.

Empty-handed, Uncle Jake was over the side in a flash.

"I was scared about that, too," I replied quietly, looking down.

"Now hold on! It ain't brave to do something you're not really afraid of. If you're scared of something and you do it anyway—that's what being brave is. This team is young and skittish. If you hadn't held 'em, they'd have wrecked the wagon, busted up the harness, and right now we'd be tramping through the bush looking for 'em.

"This silly little dog," he went on, "got himself in a peck of trouble, and you and me worked together to save him. We each had a part in it, and I want you to remember that."

It felt good, knowing that I had played an important part in saving Mopus.

I don't know how that little mutt was able to survive such an injury, but survive he did. Although it was several months before Mopus could move freely again, in time he made a full recovery. Uncle Jake was happy about that, and I sure was, too.

My Father's World

TO WRITE A BIOGRAPHY OF MY FATHER would well surpass the pages of this book. Among other things, Dad was a mechanic, an electrician, and a farmer. Although he did not go beyond grade school, he was an avid reader and had many interests. He composed a number of songs—words and music—and had some published, too. In the 1930s, he built a wind charger to provide electricity for the household. The propeller was hand carved from a birch plank.

Dad built the first bridge across the White Fox River, north of the village of White Fox, hauling the huge log stringers into place with his horses. He also brought one of the first land-breaking outfits into his area of the northeast: a 22–36 McCormick–Deering tractor and a twenty-two inch International breaking plow. He also broke up the land for many homesteaders. Later, when his health became a major problem, young Charlie Vivian ran the outfit. Between them, they broke hundreds of acres.

In the late 1930s, Dad was heavily involved in the establishment and construction of the first school in the district—Grey Fox School. It was located about a mile and three quarters north of the village of Love.

Sadly for both of us, Dad and I did not always have a close relationship in my early years. The exception to this was shooting, hunting, and the bush. We always seemed to be on the same wavelength regarding these subjects. In writing about my father, therefore, it seems natural and appropriate for me to record those things about him that I know best. After all, the edge of the wilderness was my father's world. He loved it. He chose it. He lived in it.

Dad was born Ryburn Robert Updike, on 6 November 1897, in a small community on the outskirts of Chicago, Illinois. When he was in his early teens, his parents separated. His mother moved to southern Saskatchewan with most of the children. Dad enjoyed the outdoors. He often hunted ducks and geese on the Quill Lakes. Later, he made a number of trips north to hunt big game. He was fascinated by the undeveloped frontier.

During the First World War, Dad returned to the United States, enlisted, and fought with the American Expeditionary Force in France.

When he left the army in 1918, he returned to a place far removed from the noise and horror of war—northern Saskatchewan. There, he built a log cabin and began homesteading on a quarter section of virgin forest.

Dad was highly respected as a hunter and an authority on wildlife. As far back as I can remember, every fall, men came to our place to have Dad sight-in their rifles, and to talk hunting and ask his advice. Sometimes discouraged hunters stopped by, hoping that Dad could tell them something that would help them to fill their licence. Some hunters almost pleaded with Dad to accompany them. They knew that for some reason they would find game wherever Dad went hunting.

My father hunted elk, caribou, and a lot

My father in his US Army uniform in 1918.

of deer, but most of all he liked to hunt moose. His favourite hunting rifle over the years was a .303 Ross. He especially liked its fast straight-pull bolt action. He always acknowledged that the US Army .30–06 was much superior, yet stayed with the .303. When I was young, I wondered why. Lately, I've suspected that perhaps he feared that packing a .30–06 would awaken too many painful wartime memories.

One fall afternoon just before hunting season, a few neighbours came over for some lively talk about the merits of various rifles. Some of the men were proud of the rifles they carried and very vocal about it. I was impressed and asked Dad more about the conversation later.

"A man should have a good rifle," said Dad, "best he can afford, I suppose. The quality of the rifle is not the most important thing in successful hunting, though."

"Well, what is?" I asked.

"The first requirement is to know your game. The second is to know how to hunt. The third is to know how to shoot. If a guy does well in these three areas he'll take his share of game even if he doesn't have an expensive rifle."

Dad was a superb marksman, and even in old age he possessed remarkable eyesight. He was an excellent hunter and was extremely knowledgeable in the bush. But he told me of a time when it wasn't always that way, when he was losing confidence in both his rifle and his ability in the bush. Game seemed scarce, and after tramping the woods day after day and coming home empty-handed, he became discouraged.

One cold afternoon, he came upon a small Cree encampment. The Indians were happily butchering a large bull moose. Dad congratulated them on their good fortune and asked who the successful hunter was.

One of the men called to someone in a nearby tipi. Soon, a short heavy woman of perhaps forty emerged.

"Did you shoot the moose?" Dad inquired.

The woman nodded.

Dad asked what kind of a rifle she had used.

She went back into the lodge and brought out a single-shot .22 that was in very bad shape. The stock had cracked and was bound together with wrappings of brass rabbit-snare wire. The action and barrel were severely rusted. Dad thought the piece did not look safe to fire.

"How many shots?" he asked.

"One," the hunter said, holding up a stubby forefinger.

Dad asked how far away from the bull she was when she fired.

The woman was thoughtful for a few moments then replied, "Three steps."

By now Dad was thoroughly flabbergasted. He looked at the enormous bull, the small woman, and the derelict weapon. "How did you do it?" he burst out.

The dark-skinned woman reflected again for a moment. Then she told the whole amazing story in one brief sentence, "I wait ... he come ... I shoot."

Dad was embarrassed by that experience, but he learned a valuable lesson that day. He was carrying a .44–40 Winchester, a rifle he considered under-powered for large game. Compared to the Indian woman's .22, his .44–40 was a cannon. He said the realization hit home that the most important element in taking game is definitely not the kind of firearm a person carries. He knew he could really shoot, but he realized that if he was going to survive in the wilderness he had better also learn how to really hunt.

Dad learned a lot from the Indians. Most importantly, he embarked on an extensive study of

My father shows off the hind leg of a very large moose.

66

the wilderness and its creatures that was to last more than half a lifetime. Dad became a self-taught naturalist. He studied and diligently kept journals that recorded detailed information about plants and wildlife. He examined and recorded the stomach contents of every bird and animal he killed. He knew their feeding habits for each season and how they reacted to the presence of humans.

When he explained all this to me one day later in life, I began to understand why his hunting excursions always had such predictable outcomes, and why luck and chance figured so prominently in the hunting experiences of a lot of us.

One autumn, Dad was contracted to supply wild meat to a large sawmill in the north (it was not illegal in those times). That winter he shot eight moose, several elk, and quite a few deer. He used the same .44–40 he had been unsuccessful with several years earlier. Dad was beginning to understand the wilderness and its creatures, and he was learning how to hunt.

In early times, the northern homesteaders worked at clearing their land and bringing it under cultivation in the summer. In the winter, many went south to find work. Some took to trapping or working in sawmills. One fall, Dad hired on with a guiding firm that catered to southern hunters who desired to hunt northern big game.

He told me about one wealthy American client who had hopes of bagging a trophy moose. The man had expensive equipment and a fine rifle. Around camp, he demonstrated that he was a good marksman. He talked a lot about hunting, but Dad suspected that his hunting prowess was mostly talk.

Later that week, Dad guided his client to within eighty yards of a very large bull moose with an impressive rack. Dad urged the hunter to shoot and take his trophy. The man became befuddled and excited. Finally, he got his rifle up and fired. The shot kicked up snow about ten yards off target. The bull lumbered toward the heavy bush. Dad said he then witnessed the worst case of "buck fever" he had ever seen. The hunter trembled violently; his face was flushed, and his eyes were wide and glassy. He brought his rifle up again, but instead of firing, he levered a live cartridge out into the snow.

He repeated this until he had emptied his rifle. He never fired another shot.

Dad observed that the moose was about to make cover, so he dropped the animal with one well-placed shot from his .303. The trophy hunter was not even aware that Dad had fired.

When the moose collapsed in the snow the spell was broken, and the man came to his senses. "Man, those moose are tough to bring down!" he exclaimed. "I had to empty my rifle to stop him!"

Dad never told what really happened on that hunt. The trophy hunter went home with his big bull and his even bigger story.

Over the years, my father formed some strong personal convictions about wildlife and hunting. He hunted only to put meat on the table and came to believe, as the Indians did, that those who hunt owe respect and responsibility to the animals that sustain them. No doubt this position is one reason why Dad never hunted bear, although he shot one in self-defence once. That day, Dad struck out north across the creek with his big yellow mongrel, Butch. He hadn't gone far before he wished he'd left the animal at home. Butch chased everything that moved: squirrels, rabbits, birds. At one point the dog bounded into the dense woods near the east bank of the creek.

In a short time there was the sound of fierce barking, then an ominous roar followed by small yelps from a mighty scared dog. Butch had surprised a black bear feasting in a blueberry patch, and the old boar had taken exception to the intrusion.

Dad could hear the commotion coming steadily closer from quite a distance. Then, he caught glimpses of them: a flash of yellow, then a flash of black, racing through the bush at breakneck speed. The dog darted around the thick alder bushes, and the bear crashed right through them. The dog yelped, while the bruin grunted and roared.

At first Dad thought the scene was kind of humorous. Then, as the two animals broke into the clearing along the edge of the creek bank, he realized what was about to happen. The frightened dog was going to flee to his master—with a five-hundred-pound bear not twenty feet behind.

Dad yelled at the top of his voice and waved his arms. No sir! That black would not back down. At the last moment, Dad levelled the .303 and fired at point-blank range. Three or four yards from Dad's feet, the bear hit the ground and tumbled over the bank. He rolled and flopped through the straggly brush all the way to the valley floor. There, he rose to full height on his hind legs and waved his right foreleg, roaring angrily at the man and the yellow dog who peered down the steep slope at him. His left foreleg dangled uselessly. Dad felt badly that the animal had to be destroyed. He never took a dog with him into the bush again.

Early in my father's homestead days, he was awakened about midnight by the horses stomping and whinnying in the barn. Alarmed, and perhaps not fully awake, he jumped out of bed, pulled on his pants, and made for the door.

In northern Saskatchewan, summer nights are often not totally dark. This was such a night, and there was just enough light to dimly recognize shapes. As Dad reached the front door, he was startled by the bulky form of René Blais, a neighbour who homesteaded five miles to the west. "René, what are you doing here?" Dad asked.

The big Frenchman stood silently for a moment then, with a loud grunt, dropped down on all fours and quickly disappeared into the bush. It wasn't René at all but an inquisitive black bear paying a midnight call.

Although there was no excuse for Dad's case of mistaken identity, René was a heavily built former wrestler, and in the semi-darkness the bear's ears looked exactly like the big homesteader's fishing hat with the brim turned up at both sides.

My Uncle Ted once told me a story that illustrates my father's unusual hunting and shooting prowess. The two brothers were deer hunting along the Fern Creek, and while Dad stayed on the south bank, Uncle Ted descended into the valley. In a short time, five deer fled the valley and climbed the north bank, directly across from my father's position. As they reached the top of the far bank—why carry the carcasses up a steep bank?—Dad opened fire.

My uncle said he thought he heard five shots, but the echo that reverberated through that valley sounded like a military bombardment. When it was finally silent, he called out from below, "Are you through?"

"Yep!" his older brother hollered back.

When the two hunters climbed up the far bank, they found five deer lying in an area no more than forty feet across. Each had been felled cleanly with a single shot.

Uncle Ted said he remembered muttering to himself as he surveyed the scene, "I don't know how he does that."

The hunt was successful and the brothers made sure that more than half the meat ended up on a lot of other tables in the community.

I have come to the conclusion that men who have developed their wilderness and wildlife skills to very high levels not only possess wisdom and keen insights, but that they also have a special instinct about the wild—a unique inner knowledge that most of us who have lived in the wilderness do not possess. I often observed this innate sense in my father, but one incident that took place when I was about ten is particularly clear in my memory.

It was autumn, and our family was visiting another farm family a few miles to the north. Later in the evening, two young men, mutual friends, stopped by. They announced that they had brought their rifles and intended to drive to some nearby fields and see if they could jacklight a deer. They were eager to have Dad accompany them.

Dad vigorously opposed the illegal practice and tried to discourage the young men. After a lengthy conversation, Dad agreed to go along but said he would not participate. I didn't understand why he consented but I was excited because I got to go too.

Dad suggested the alfalfa field, the south side near the bush. The young driver followed his advice, and as if by magic there they were, four deer feeding near the heavy bush at the south edge of the field. The animals were transfixed. They milled around a little but just couldn't take their eyes off the glaring headlights.

We approached slowly to a range of about fifty yards. The hunters jumped out, knelt beside the front fenders and blazed away. The deer finally scattered and drifted into the bush.

"Damn!" the driver said. "We never even touched 'em."

"Drive up there," my father directed.

We drove quickly to where the deer had been.

"Cut your lights and wait here," Dad said.

To everyone's amazement, Dad got out and, without a word, disappeared into the pitch-black bush. The two jacklighters began to speculate about where Dad had gone and what he was doing in the dark.

After about ten minutes, we heard a low whistle. The driver flicked on his lights to reveal Dad standing at the edge of the field, waving us over. We followed him about twenty yards into the thick bush. There lay a young yearling buck. Dad had bled it with his pocketknife.

The hunters packed the young animal out to the car, loaded it in the trunk, and returned to the neighbour's farm. They hung the deer in a shed behind the barn.

"Well, Ryburn," one hunter said, "this is really your deer. We didn't even know we'd hit one, and we couldn't have found it, anyway."

Dad said he wanted nothing to do with the deer and proceeded to give the young hunters a stern lecture about the folly of jacklighting. They agreed and vowed to give up the practice.

On the way home my young mind was in a whirl. "Dad," I said, "how did you know that buck was hit? And how did you know where he went? And how could you find him in the dark?"

"Ah, well," he drawled, "I just saw he was hit and followed him. It's not totally dark, you know. Your eyes adjust."

I've never understood how Dad was able to do that. I can only attribute it to some kind of highly developed instinct. Perhaps it's best to agree with Uncle Ted and say, "I don't know how he does that."

From the time I was very young until I left home at seventeen, Dad and I talked a lot about hunting, shooting, and the bush. Whenever folks complimented me about my shooting skills, I always said, "My dad taught me that." Though, in the end, I could match Dad at close-range shooting, when it came to hunting I wasn't even in his league. Everything worthwhile I did learn about hunting, though, came from him.

The years have gone and so has my dad. He has long been with the Lord he trusted. And I, appropriately I suppose, have fallen heir to his old .303 Ross. I unwrap it now and again and work the heavy bolt action that he handled so expertly. I squint through those iron sights, and I remember.

That rifle hasn't fired a shot in forty years. The once-blued steel of the barrel and action is worn and discoloured. The oiled hardwood of the stock is mottled with stain and has many a scratch. Somehow, though, I have an affection for that old rifle. It is a poignant reminder of the early years of my life, when things were the best between my dad and me, and of how life once was in my father's world.

Hard Times on the Homestead

"IS DAD DYING, MOM?" I ASKED. "Is he dying this time?"

"I don't know, Son," my mom replied. "I really don't know." As she spoke, it sounded like each word required a special effort. "I want you to go to Uncle Jake's and ask him to come right away to take Dad to the hospital."

"I'll run all the way," I said, grabbing my cap.

"No, no," she said. "Please hurry, but don't run all the way."

I bolted out the door and down the bush trail to the grid road that passed by Uncle Jake's place, one mile west. I did run all the way and straight into the house. It was mid-afternoon, and Grandma, Aunt Lena, and Uncle Jake were having coffee when I burst in.

"Uncle Jake," I gasped, "Dad is having a very bad sick spell, dying maybe. Mom wants you to please come right away to take him to the hospital."

"Sure thing," my big uncle replied. "C'mon, let's go!" He rose immediately and was at the door in a couple of strides.

I wasn't crying, but rivulets of tears wouldn't stop coursing down my cheeks.

"Boy, you're out of puff," he said. "Bet you ran all the way, huh?"

I nodded.

We climbed into Uncle Jake's big McLaughlin-Buick and rumbled out of the yard at a good clip. It's true that nobody ever accused my uncle of being a slow and cautious driver, but that day he had the old Buick pushed to the limit. It felt like we were flying over the dirt road, and in no time we careened into our yard.

Uncle Jake jumped out and went quickly into the house.

I tagged along at his heels and followed him right into my parents' bedroom.

I was staggered by what I saw in the tiny, sparsely furnished bedroom that afternoon. My Dad, normally a strong, controlled man, lay writhing and moaning on the bed. His face was flushed and puffy. In his delirium, he seemed to be reliving the horror of some wartime experience. "I tore at him with my bayonet," he cried, "but he was so scared!"

I trembled in fear, certain that my dad was on his deathbed. I looked at Mom. Her face was pale and drawn, but I could see a hidden strength that only comes to those who have faced many hardships in their lives without ever abandoning hope.

"He won't survive the trip by car," Uncle Jake said to Mom. "I'll go to Nipawin and get Doc Scott as fast as I can. He'll send the ambulance." He turned on his heel. In a moment, the car door slammed and the Buick roared down the driveway.

"I want you to look after your brother until the ambulance takes your dad away," said Mom. "Take him for a walk somewhere away from the yard, please."

I took Harley, my five-year-old brother, across the road to

My parents on their wedding day, 1 June 1929.

an abandoned log house. After the ambulance arrived, then left at high speed, we returned. Mom was sitting in the kitchen alone.

"The doctor says there is nothing I can do now," she said. "Uncle Jake will take me in to see Dad this evening."

Dad had a history of debilitating illness for as long as I could remember. A stomach ulcer had perforated several times. The diagnosis this time was that something more serious had developed. The doctors suspected cancer. It was determined that Dad required major surgery—the kind of surgery that could not be performed in a small-town hospital and maybe not even in Regina. At any rate, we had no money for such a costly procedure.

After some quick letters and a number of phone calls, Dr. Scott discovered that Veteran's Affairs in the United States would cover all costs if Dad could get to Hines Military Hospital in Chicago.

It was Uncle Jake, again, and Uncle Frank who were there to help. They canvassed the community on Dad's behalf and collected enough money from friends and neighbours to finance the trip.

A few weeks later, Dad departed for his home state. He underwent extensive but successful surgery. Recovery time and subsequent radiation treatment kept him south of the border for nearly eight months.

There was never any shortage of work at the edge of the wilderness on our homestead. With Dad away, my responsibilities seemed almost overwhelming; at age thirteen, it was time for me to become a man, and there was much to do.

First, I had to ensure that we had a supply of firewood adequate to outlast the long winter. It took many weeks with a swede saw and axe to cut a full supply for winter. I sure was proud of the giant pile of logs I hauled in with the Fordson tractor and our small trailer. Then I made arrangements for a few neighbours to come one Saturday and saw the logs into stove-sized blocks.

The farming operation produced the majority of our meagre finances. There was a small crop of wheat ripening nicely on the south field. Charlie harvested it for us with his small combine. The trapline contributed some money as well.

I shot squirrels and trapped weasels. I even trapped two mink on Fern Creek that winter. The money that came from that year's trapping endeavour wasn't a lot, but anything that made a difference in our cash flow was welcome.

Hunting, growing, gathering, and preserving our food supply was a year-round occupation. Every summer Mom, my sister Jean, and I spent many hours picking wild fruit to be preserved for winter in glass jars called sealers. The first berries to ripen were the raspberries and strawberries, followed by the saskatoons. Blueberries came in August, along with the patches of red and black currants and high-bush cranberries that flourished on the creek banks. If the wind was right, you could smell their pungent aroma for a hundred yards. Pin cherries, chokecherries, and low-bush cranberries abounded nearby. Usually by fall, Mom would count upwards of a hundred quart jars of fruit preserves on shelves in the cellar. The year Dad was recuperating from his operation was no exception.

My mother was a small, cheerful woman from a Mennonite background. She worked hard all her life, and she taught us by example that work could be fun. We could laugh and encourage one another while working, even as we were wholly involved in the tasks critical to our own survival. Jean and I willingly pitched in and tried our best to face work the same way that Mom did.

Mom was a remarkable gardener. She had an innate sense of how to make things grow. Every spring, she planted a huge garden—far larger than we needed. She always said, "Someone else might not have enough, and maybe we can help." Nobody left our place empty-handed. There was always a jar of jam or a pail of fresh-picked peas or a loaf of homemade bread ready to give away. Despite Mom's generosity, there was always enough left for us. Every fall the shelves and bins in our cellar were loaded with fruit and garden produce.

Starting at age seven, I took at least a month off school in the fall to help with harvest and preparation for winter. Consequently, my school year began sometime in October. It was tough, but the teachers usually understood, and by Christmas I'd be caught up with the rest of the class. That year, with Dad in Chicago, keeping up with my studies seemed tougher than usual.

We had one milk cow and two yearlings that year, and the cow provided enough milk to get by on. Mom always kept a sizable flock of chickens, which kept us in eggs most of the winter. But each time Mom thought we needed something special for Sunday dinner, the flock diminished.

I made regular forays into the woods with the .22 to replenish our meat supply. I brought home a lot of grouse and rabbits. It isn't difficult to keep meat frozen when the temperature frequently drops to forty below zero. Our deep-freeze was a granary behind the shop.

When winter fully set in, the bush trail from the yard to the main road quickly drifted over with snow. Charlie plowed it out occasionally, but it didn't matter much because we didn't have a vehicle. We walked the four miles to the village of Love and carried home the supplies we needed. I made the eight-mile round trip once or twice a week with Mom or Jean. But groceries were seldom the prime reason for a trip to town. There were always letters to mail to Dad, and our first stop was the post office. We'd read mail from Dad right there before we went to the general store.

When winter arrived early, vegetables were dug from a cold and snowy garden.

That was a hard year in many ways. Late one night, I woke up and heard someone softly crying. It was Mom. I made my way downstairs in the chill of the old farmhouse. The lamp was burning in Mom's room. I knocked quietly and went in. "What's wrong, Mom?" I whispered.

"Oh, I'm just so lonely and worried about your dad," she said, wiping her eyes. "I'm afraid he's never coming back."

I sat on the edge of the bed and took her hand. "I'm lonely and worried too, Mom," I said, "but Dad's going to be all right. He's had his surgery and he's getting stronger, and he's in the best hospital there is. You'll see; he's going to get well and come home soon. Don't cry, Mom. It's tough on us all, but we're going to make it."

"Oh, I know you're right, Son," Mom said, looking a little brighter. "I'm just being silly, but I just felt so lonely tonight I couldn't help crying. I'm okay now. You cheered me up real good."

"Should I light the stove and make some tea?" I asked.

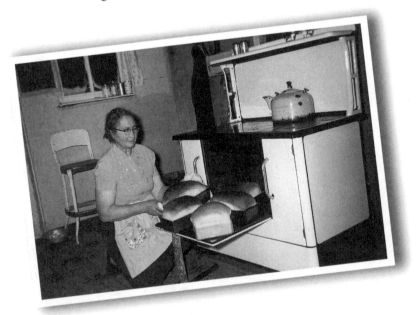

Mom always had a loaf of homemade bread, a jar of jam, or a pail of fresh-picked peas ready to give to visitors.

"My word, no!" she replied. "I'm fine now. You go back to bed, and don't be worrying about me, either."

As I lay on my straw-tick mattress and stared up at the darkness that night, I wasn't so sure I really believed everything I had told my mother. But it had to work out; it just had to.

Another night, I was jolted awake by a roaring sound that seemed to fill my small bedroom. I leaped out of bed and ran to the window. A red glow bathed the snow-covered yard, and as I realized what was happening, fear made the chill of the room feel like forty below. The stovepipes and the chimney were on fire. I fumbled for a match and lit my coal-oil lamp. The roar increased in a frightening crescendo.

The stovepipes venting the cook stove and airtight heater passed up through the floor in my room and elbowed into the concrete chimney. When fuelling such a setup with resin-loaded pine, it is necessary to clean the chimney and stovepipes frequently. If this task is neglected, soot and combustible residue, which can ignite and burn with fierce intensity, will build up. With an increasing feeling of dread, I realized that I had forgotten to clean the stovepipes.

"The chimney's on fire!" I yelled as I yanked on my clothes. I hammered on Jean's door on the way downstairs. "Get dressed and get downstairs right away. The chimney's on fire!"

Mom was already dressed and had the lamps lit. Bewildered and frightened, she asked, "What'll we do?"

I realized that danger to the house was extreme and that immediate action was critical. It was also very clear that I was the only one present who could take charge. I wasn't sure I could handle it, but there was no alternative to consider. I tried to dismiss my fears and resolved to do everything I could to save the house.

I'd seen a chimney fire a year and a half before. I had helped Dad combat it, and I remembered what he did. I closed all the dampers tight to stop the updraft as much as possible. "It starves the fire of air," Dad had said. I doused water on the fire remaining in the cook stove and airtight. I told Jean to quickly get a couple of pails of water from the well and to look after Harley when she was finished. I also told her to have everyone's coats and boots ready to leave immediately if the house caught fire. I shouted to Mom to follow me as I grabbed the water pail and headed upstairs on the run.

The stovepipes were already red hot. I was afraid they would soften and collapse, releasing the inferno into the house. I poured water on the red-hot pipes with a small dipper and trickled some down a small opening Dad had made at the top join. This let water inside the pipe. It wouldn't extinguish the fire but would create steam that could be an inhibitor.

"Keep doing this, Mom," I said, "but if anything happens and the house catches fire, leave everything and get out quick!"

"What are you going to do?" she asked.

"I gotta get on the roof and pour water down the chimney like Dad did," I answered.

"It was summer when he did that," she cried. "You can't climb that roof with a pail of water, it's too icy! It's too dangerous! My land, you're just a boy!"

"Don't worry, I can do it!" I shouted as I bounded down the stairs. I wished my confidence were as real as I pretended it was. I put on my jacket and boots in record time, picked up the second pail of water, and ran outside.

A wooden ladder nailed to the south side of the front porch provided access to the roof. After the ladder, it was an easy climb up the sloping porch roof. Dad had nailed one-by-four cleats on the house roof, two feet apart, up to the peak. I had often climbed up there in the summer but never on a winter night when the temperature was twenty-five below, never mind while carrying a pail of water.

After a harrowing climb, I reached the peak of the roof. I don't know how I did it, but fear and necessity are great motivators. I straddled the peak and worked my way toward the chimney. Like a giant blowtorch, a shaft of angry orange and red flame belched twenty feet into the night sky. The heat was searing as I drew near. I stood up shakily and dumped half the contents of the pail right into the roaring flame. Thinking I could see a difference, I dumped the rest.

There was no time for analysis. I chucked the pail over the edge and began retracing my steps. I made it down okay and ran inside and up the stairs.

"It's quieted a little," Mom said. She was calm again.

"Keep doin' what you're doin,' Mom," I said, and hit the stairs.

I grabbed a pail of water that Jean had just brought in and tackled the roof again. The blaze had abated somewhat, but was still a frightening spectacle. I sloshed the full pail down the chimney at once. The flames calmed immediately. The fire still licked a few feet into the darkness, but the fierce roar was silenced.

I perched on the roof for a while, wondering whether the fire would flare up again. It didn't. The blaze flickered more and more feebly before finally retreating down the chimney. Again, it was a cold quiet winter night in the north. I threw the pail over the side, gingerly descended the icy steps, and went inside.

I climbed the stairs slowly this time. "It's finally over," Mom said. "Thank God we didn't lose the house!"

"Yeah ... thank God," I replied.

"I was afraid the house was going to burn to the ground," she said. "I didn't know what to do."

"I was scared, too," I said. "I just did what I saw Dad do the last time the chimney caught fire."

"Well, your dad couldn't have handled it any better than you did!" Mom exclaimed.

Suddenly I felt very tired and a little shaky.

"I'm going to get the fires going again," I said.

"Good," Mom replied, "and I'm going to fix a lunch."

Jean had taken Harley back to bed, and he was tucked in and asleep.

In a short time, the fires were burning cheerily. Mom served tea, toast, and raspberry jam. Then she brought out the cookies: the big ones with the sawtooth edges and a dusting of sugar on top.

"Oh boy," I said. "Can I have two?"

"Tonight, Son," Mom replied, "you can finish the whole jar if you want to."

In those early days, hard times on the homestead were not uncommon, but that winter was the toughest I can remember.

Later that winter, Dad came home; it was a red-letter day. Of course it was a tremendous relief and joy to our family. It was also an encouragement to the whole community, for few expected Dad would ever recover and return.

Although he never regained his robust strength, Dad never again had to battle constant pain. Mom said our prayers had been answered. No doubt she was right.

The Meal I Can Never Forget

MOST FOLKS EAT ABOUT A THOUSAND MEALS A YEAR—
that's a whole lotta eatin'. When I count up all the snows
I've seen, I realize I've sat down at the table more than sixty
thousand times. Some of those meals were truly outstanding,
and I remember fondly the special meals at special times in
special places with special people. Despite my many meal
memories, there is one meal that seems to be in a class by
itself: the meal I can never forget. I did not enjoy this eating
experience in a fine restaurant in Montreal or Toronto, but in a
log cabin in the northern bush.

At fourteen, I became good friends with Fred Culhane, a
northern trapper who lived near our farm. We often hunted
together when Fred was not on the trapline.

One fall, early in the deer season, Fred and I had had a
long, frustrating day in the bush. Everything went wrong. We
spooked deer several times but didn't even get to fire a shot.
We stopped for a dry sandwich at noon and then continued,
hopeful that our luck would soon change.

Just before dusk, we were closing in on three whitetails,
and we decided to split up. Fred went left around a small
clearing, while I went right. Fred hadn't been gone ten minutes
when, across the clearing, three white flags of the fleeing deer
signalled our final failure for the day.

Disappointed, frustrated, tired, and now realizing that
I was absolutely famished, I began shuffling back to our
meeting point.

Suddenly, two grouse exploded from the grass with a whirr
of wings. They perched in a Jack pine, about fifteen feet up.
I didn't pause long to reason. It was bird season, and I had

a licence. I raised my 25–20 Winchester and decapitated the birds with a couple of quick shots.

Fred is going to think I've got a deer, I mused. I sat on a log and waited. In a short time, I spotted movement in the bush to the south. It was Fred jogging in my direction. I stood up and waved.

"Did you get one?" he asked eagerly.

"Two," I grinned.

"Two! Great! Where are they?" he asked, glancing around excitedly.

I nodded toward the two birds lying in the grass.

Fred stared. A look of disappointment replaced his jubilation. He seemed to deflate. At last he straightened up and started to laugh. "Yeah!" he said. "Why not? There'll be deer out here tomorrow and next week. Right now we're both starved and there's supper." The little trapper was excited again. "Here's what we'll do," he said. "I'll take the pa'tridge to the cabin, get 'em cleaned, and get a fire going. You go home and ask your Mom for two or three tomatoes and a couple of good-sized onions. I have potatoes."

I hurried the mile and a half home and explained to Mom what we were doing. She gave me the vegetables, a loaf of fresh homemade bread, and a jar of butter, too.

By the time I arrived at the cabin, Fred had things well under way. Four breast pieces and lots of thinly sliced potatoes were sizzling in a big iron skillet. He sliced the tomatoes and onions, and cooked the whole meal together in one pan. He didn't tell me what seasonings he added besides salt and pepper, but soon the pungent aroma from that pan filled the cabin. I don't know what part delectable odours play in helping to generate appetite, but that day their influence was overpowering.

Fred toasted thick slices of bread over open coals—the northern version of Texas toast—and he brewed strong tea in a jam pail.

It seemed like forever before supper was finally dished up, but at last we sat down before two large tin plates.

Why should one meal stand out above a lifetime of so many eating experiences? I'm not sure I know, but I'm certain it's more than just the food. No doubt the meal I enjoyed so

"Fred," I said finally, "that's the best meal I've ever had."

long ago was done to perfection. The rich flavour of the meat lifted the blandness of the potatoes. The tang of the tomatoes blended with the sharpness of the onions to enhance the juicy breast pieces. The spices tied it all together wonderfully. At the precise moment it was ready, it was served.

I also remember that I was ravenously hungry that evening, after a full day of steady activity in the great outdoors. As well, I now know that the physical senses of youth are unsurpassed. No one can experience hunger more keenly or enjoy food more fully than a healthy, active young person.

Fred and I didn't talk much through the meal—we just ate. Later, we sat back in the handmade wooden chairs, drank tea, and discussed where we would hunt the next day. The warm flickering glow of the coal-oil lamp cast grotesque shadows on the log walls. It was a good evening.

"Fred," I said finally, "that's the best meal I've ever had."

Fred was pleased, and I know he enjoyed supper, too, but obviously that wasn't his greatest meal. "Before the week is over we'll be sitting down to deer steak," he said between sips of tea. "That will be even better."

I have eaten so many meals since then. Some of them have been fabulous, but still that one stands out in my memory. No one knows the future; perhaps my greatest meal is yet to be served. Somehow, I doubt it.

Jumbo Jacks the Hard Way

IT WAS OVERCAST THAT AFTERNOON on the White Fox. The mosquitoes were relentless. "C'mon Fred," I called to my partner. "Let's call it a day. I've had enough of these mosquitoes."

Fred was reluctant. He seemed intent on fishing one spot only. "There's a whale of a fish in there," he finally confided. "He's been playing with my hook for half an hour."

We had been fishing at Munn's place, just upstream from a large beaver dam.

I watched the older man flip his red and white daredevil across the stream and troll it through deep water. Suddenly, a fish hit his lure so hard it almost tore the pole out of his hands. Moments later, a huge jackfish leaped clear of the water trying to throw the hook. "By Jove, it looks like a muskie!" Fred whooped. It was easily the largest pike either of us had ever seen.

Fred's line sliced left then moved straight for the deepest water just above the dam, and then it doubled back and whipped upstream. The small man raced along the water's edge, his pole bowed dangerously. At last, the fish veered left and headed back toward the dam. Fred was using a long slender pole with a fixed line and no reel. As a result, he was forced to run back and forth along the water's edge in order to play this powerful fish.

Northern pike generally put up a ferocious but brief battle when hooked. This monster was not only full of fight, but he also had staying power. Fred was thoroughly bushed when he finally manoeuvred his catch toward a sloping sandbar. He yelled for me to come and help him land it.

Carefully, he drew that enormous northern into shallow water. The jack seemed strangely docile as the old fisherman gently pulled him in.

Then, in dismay, I watched the hook slowly straighten and ... snap! The big pike lay in a few inches of water, unaware that he was free.

"Get 'im! Grab 'im! Do something!" Fred hollered hoarsely.

I plunged in and, to my surprise, managed to grab the fish behind the gills. As I attempted to lift him out of the water, something triggered inside that creature. He exploded in a frenzy of wild thrashing that was so powerful I was knocked off my feet.

Now in three feet of water, I wrestled with everything I had to maintain a grip on that slippery bundle of green dynamite. With every movement, we were slanting toward deeper water. Somehow, I righted myself and shoved the fish hard against the bottom. I straddled him and held on for the strangest ride of my life.

The view below the dam at Munn's place, where we caught the jumbo jacks.

The coarse sand of the river bottom at shore gradually gave way to a slippery black muck that sloped more and more sharply into deeper water. My underwater mount and I were heading rapidly toward the depths. It didn't take long to realize that I could not conquer this fish in his element. I had to get him into mine, and quickly, or give up and let him go.

Renewing my grip one more time, I lurched to my feet and heaved the fish to arm's length overhead. He barely cleared the surface and writhed furiously as I struggled to remain upright. Finally, in desperation, I flung him toward the shore as hard as I could. He landed there and flopped in the grass.

While Fred shouted from the shore, I staggered chest-deep in the White Fox, fully clothed and totally soaked. "Wow!" I gasped. "What a fish!"

We couldn't believe our eyes. That pike was enormous. Fred was right; it did look like a muskellunge. We didn't have a scale large enough to accommodate our catch, but he taped out at thirty-eight and a half inches. It was clearly the largest jackfish ever taken from the White Fox in anyone's recent memory.

Fred and I joked about who actually caught the whopper. I guess we both did, and that was the only fish I ever caught with my bare hands. Though it was well worth it, I'll be the first to admit that it's a hard way to catch fish. Dad took a few snapshots to record our contribution to local fishing history.

The story of successfully fishing for jackfish in the White Fox River began in the early 1940s. At that time, several colonies of beavers migrated downstream from the west. In a few years, the industrious animals had built a number of dams in our area. The water level rose dramatically, revitalizing the whole valley. Fish that were spawned upriver were hindered by dams and could not return downstream to the Torch and Saskatchewan Rivers. The White Fox was transformed from a shallow, algae-covered stream into a vibrant river, well stocked with fish—mostly northern pike.

There had never been a lot of fishing in the White Fox, even after the beavers came. The stream was hard to access because of the heavy growth of trees and willows that grew almost to the edge of the water in most places. But in the summer of 1948, an American taught us how to fish our own river. Fred had a rancher cousin in Wyoming named Hugh. Hugh spent six weeks with Fred that summer. The Yank knew a lot about a lot of things, and fishing certainly was one of them.

The cousins fished the Saskatchewan and the Torch, but Hugh wanted to fish the White Fox. We explained that, because of the profusion of trees and brush along the banks, fishing with rod and reel would be frustrating at best.

Hugh puffed his pipe thoughtfully and said in his Wyoming drawl, "They's piiike in that river, miiiighty big piiiike. If we gotta use poles to catch 'em, we'll use poles."

The next day Fred and Hugh visited the White Fox. They cut long, slender willow poles and attached a good length of twenty-pound test line to each pole. Selecting medium to heavy spinners and daredevils, they fished. That day, they hauled in so many pike they had enough to share with the neighbours. Most of the fish were northern pike: jackfish, or "jacks," as folks up there call them.

Soon, many local residents became interested in the pole method of fishing for pike. It was primitive, but it worked. In a short time, a lot of nice jackfish were sizzling in a lot of frying pans in our community.

Even Fred and I laid aside our conventional tackle in favour of the "pole and troll" method of fishing for jacks and continued it after Hugh had gone back across the forty-ninth. Although we caught

Fred and me with our impressive catch.

some large fish from time to time, none came close to the giant we landed that day at Munn's.

Three days after our impressive catch, I had a hankering to fish at Munn's again. Fred wasn't feeling well, so I went alone. I returned to the spot where Fred had stood to hook his big one. I recalled that he had let his lure sink much deeper than usual that day. I made a few casts, trolling slowly and permitting the spinner to sink deeply.

Before I had trailed the spinner through that spot a dozen times, a dark form shot out of the depths and nailed my lure just as it broke the surface. It looked like the same enormous fish we had taken from the same waters just three days before. I thought history only repeated itself in fiction. This was real— and there he was!

I never experienced anything in fishing quite like the savagery of that huge jackfish as he attempted to break free. Now it was my turn to race back and forth along the water's edge. Several times, I feared my pole would snap because of the sheer force of the pike's wild acrobatics. After about twenty minutes, I was feeling pretty winded, but I guessed that the fish must have been running out of gas as well. Gradually, his movements slowed. I began to wonder how I would land him, alone and without a net. Then I thought of the spillway on the dam. Maybe I could get him heading downstream and sluice him over the dam onto the sticks below.

It took a lot of careful pole handling to condition that fish to be drawn up to the spillway then to turn slowly back toward the deeper water. I turned him to the mouth of the spillway one more time and jumped quickly onto the dam. Gradually, I increased his speed. When he was a few yards out, I yanked hard, hoping the treble hook and heavy line wouldn't let go. They held. He shot through the spillway like a green torpedo. I leaped the six feet to the base of the dam and in a moment had a huge jackfish trapped on the bleached white sticks.

I was elated at this second stroke of unbelievably good fishing fortune—all within three days. I took off for Fred's place immediately, anxious to show him the latest whopper. Out of selfishness, no doubt, I secretly hoped it would measure larger than the first one. Alas, it taped a full inch shorter: a measly thirty-seven and a half inches.

I was a kid of sixteen then and I have had a full creel of good fishing experiences since. None, however, quite measure up to those exciting days on the White Fox, fishing for jumbo jacks the hard way.

Tough Choices

HIS BIG FIST HAMMERED INTO MY FACE. The impact was numbing, driving me to both knees on the icy road. I lurched up and waded in, swinging with both hands. A looping right pounded teeth through my bottom lip. The blows just kept coming.

I don't remember how many times I was thrown and knocked to the ground that day. At last, I was just too uncoordinated to make it to my feet and return to the fray.

For a few minutes I lay on the road, disoriented and oblivious to the twenty-below-zero temperature. Even the pain and humiliation were overshadowed by the question—why? Why would a guy beat up a friend like this?

Although Reggie and I had the occasional scrap when we were boys, our fights were quickly forgotten. I didn't understand what was happening now. I was nearly fourteen. Reg, a year and a half older, had matured quickly. He was a young man out in the workforce. He looked old enough to enter hotel beverage rooms and frequently did. In comparison to him, I was still a kid.

As I watched my own blood trickle down and melt into the snow, a dark anger began to smoulder. Then, a very strange thing happened. From somewhere deep inside, I heard a voice that sounded a lot like my own saying, "This will never happen again!" Those words resonated inside me with such finality that I didn't question their truth for a moment. Immediately, I got to my feet and began the two-mile walk home. Somehow I felt different. This was the day I made a tough choice that would profoundly affect my young life.

Long before I reached my teens, I had come to hate being poor. At times I resented how our extreme poverty affected me personally. Mostly though, I felt bad for my parents and especially for my mother.

Our farm had never produced enough to adequately meet our family's needs. The Great Depression of the 1930s, followed by Dad's persistent illness, were giant blows from which we never fully recovered. We were in need of seemingly unavailable major financing in order to make the farm a viable operation.

I often thought about how I might be able to contribute to the family coffers. I had a natural talent for drawing. I sometimes wondered if becoming a successful artist would help me to make enough money to meet the family's needs. It seemed very uncertain.

And then there was boxing. I had always been fascinated by the sport. Dad boxed in the army. Uncle Ted was a boxer. I had scrapbooks filled with boxing pictures and information. I had a distant but persistent dream of one day becoming a renowned boxer—maybe even a champion. What an achievement that would be! Surely it would put an end to poverty in our family.

Then the impossible happened. Fred Culhane, a career trapper from Manitoba, purchased a trapline in the north from my Uncle Ted. Fred was a former professional boxer. As Fred and I hunted and fished together, we talked a lot about boxing.

One day I asked Fred if he would train me to be a boxer.

"No," he replied quickly, "at least I hope not."

"But why not?" I burst out in surprise.

"Because you're too intelligent, and you're too nice a kid," he said. "You should be studying to be a doctor, or a lawyer, or an artist, or something, not considering the fight game. Boxing is a tough, dirty business," he continued. "It's full of corruption, and the higher you go, the worse it gets."

"Hmm ... well ... just thought I'd ask," I mumbled.

"Hey," Fred laughed. "I didn't mean to preach at you. It's just that boxing is not something you dabble at; it requires an all-out commitment. Deciding to be a boxer is a tough choice, one that you need to be sure about. Are you ready for that kind of a decision?" he asked.

"Well, maybe not," I answered. "I'm kind of unsure about a few things."

"That's good," Fred responded. "It indicates that boxing

At seventeen, I was six feet tall, weighed 160 pounds, and was an extremely well-conditioned athlete eager to face the challenges that lay ahead.

is not for you; at least not now. If things change in the next couple of years, we'll talk."

In the months that followed, my older friend and I did not discuss the subject of me becoming a boxer. Although I pondered the idea a lot, I came to no firm conclusion.

As I trudged home that afternoon after my encounter with Reggie, I recalled my conversation with Fred. "If things change ..." he'd said. I spat blood in the snow. Things have changed, I thought, and this will never happen again. My choice was finally clear.

I waited for more than a week before going to Fred's place. The cuts and bruises had mostly healed by then.

"I've been worried about you," The older man said. "This sort of thing shouldn't happen. He outweighs you by forty pounds."

"What's hard to handle is—why?" I replied.

"Life's been tough for Reg," he said. "Maybe you just happened to be there when he felt like getting even."

"Yeah, I suppose it's something like that," I said. "Anyway, I'm trying to let it go."

"Good," he replied. Fred brewed a pot of strong tea and we sat in the warm glow of the coal-oil lamp. He was spending a few weeks away from the trapline, recovering from a recurrent bowel problem.

I finally got to what was really on my mind. I explained that while I was hurt and humiliated by the pounding I had taken from Reg, it had nevertheless helped me to a decision. I told him that things had changed, and I wanted to get into the fight game.

Fred was cautious and thoughtful. He wanted to know exactly why I thought I should be in boxing. "Getting beat up by a guy twice your size is not a good enough reason," he said.

"We've always been poor," I began. "My dad has been sick as long as I can remember. For years, he hasn't been able to work like he wanted and needed to. Since his cancer surgery, I've had to quit school and work the farm full time. I'd like to further my education," I continued, "but I can't. At least not now. I'd like to study art, but there's no money for it. I'm stuck here for at least three or four more years, until my brothers are old enough to help on the farm. If you train me for those three or four years," I went on, "when I move to the city I should be able to get fights right away. I think it could work. From my perspective, boxing might be my best chance to accomplish something and help my family, too."

Fred stroked his chin thoughtfully, "I can see you've given this a lot of thought. And you very well might have what it takes to make it big as a fighter. There are many other factors though that can make or break a career. It's a long shot. Only a small percentage of boxers actually make big money."

My older friend sat back and shared some history of his experiences in the fight game. He talked of broken promises, dishonest managers, and crooked promoters. His father had been Heavyweight Champion of England, and young Fred had grown up rubbing shoulders with world champions. At the peak of his career, Fred had been a world-class lightweight. Later, he trained and managed some top-ranked boxers. At last, disillusioned, he stepped away from the sport entirely.

"The dark side of boxing will be no more palatable for you than it was for me," he said, "but it's a reality you have to face if you're going to box."

"Yeah," I replied. "I guess that's why a guy needs a good manager."

He nodded, then he pointed out that some of the toughest decisions a professional athlete must face have to do with personal things—the social life, for instance. Going to parties and dances, developing relationships with girls, getting engaged, getting married—all are normal pursuits for most guys. But they don't fit into the life of a guy battling his way up the fistic ladder. "Remember," he said, "soft kisses are more dangerous to a boxing career than hard punches are." Fred sat back and folded his arms as though he had said all he intended to say on the subject.

Neither of us spoke for some time. My mind sifted through weighty thoughts. "Y'know, Fred," I said finally, "being raised in the bush with no opportunity to improve yourself, working as hard as you can year after year, and still seeing your family in poverty is kind of tough, too."

"You're damn right it is," he agreed quickly.

"I see what you're trying to make me understand," I said, "but, in spite of everything that's wrong with boxing, it isn't just a battle to survive, it's a battle to achieve something. There's a chance to get somewhere! It's a tough choice but I've made it."

"Now, Fred," I asked soberly, "what do you choose? Will you train me?"

"Yes, I will," he responded. "I guess I was hoping you wouldn't make this choice. But now that you have, yes, I would consider it an honour to train you and later on to be your manager." We shook hands to seal our agreement. The rest of the evening was filled with excited talk about the career we planned to shape together.

As I walked home, I knew I was different. There was a sureness and confidence in each stride that I had not experienced before. New hope and a clear purpose were already working a transformation.

The next day, Fred and I got started. With Dad's help, we fixed up a rough gym in our garage. The heavy bag was a canvas alfalfa sack filled with oats. There wasn't room to install the light bag inside so we attached a platform to an outside wall. Later, I thought I must be the only aspiring boxer in Canada who could be found punching the speed bag outdoors on a January afternoon at thirty below zero.

"We've got lots of time," my new trainer said, "which means you'll be able to master all the fundamentals thoroughly. And something else: both of us are going to have some fun!" Fred was as excited about our new venture as I was. I guessed that our plans had brought a new sense of purpose to his life as well.

We talked long about the style of fighter I would become, or "the blueprint," as Fred called it. "I'm tall and slender like Sugar Ray Robinson," I said. "I think my style should be similar to his; you know, a slick boxer with a punch but able to stand toe to toe and fight when necessary."

"Well, yeah," Fred agreed, "except I don't want to see a lot of this toe-to-toe stuff. Leave that for the guys who can't learn anything else. You've got the brains, better to use 'em than to have 'em scrambled.

"There's one more thing I'd like to add," he continued, "in fact, I insist on it. I want to train you to have the best left jab in the business. It takes years to learn properly, but if you master it, it almost puts you in a class by yourself."

"Wow, I'm all for that!" I exclaimed.

My trainer proved to be a master of every phase of boxing and knew how to teach it. He had the happy knack of combining relentless perfectionism with lots of patience and good-natured enthusiasm. Though I didn't fully realize it at the time, I was receiving world-class training right there in the northern bush.

At first, I felt dumb and awkward, but I still threw everything I had into every workout. And Fred was right; it was fun. In spite of the sweat and pain, we both had fun, and I began to really learn.

With Fred, everything had to be "right," every move, every position, every punch. It was tedious and gruelling, but the discipline proved to be invaluable in years to come.

He continually stressed the importance of well-conditioned legs and good footwork. Consequently, I ran a lot of miles, skipped a lot of rope, and learned great footwork from a great teacher.

Right from the outset, it was apparent that my trainer was deadly serious about equipping me with the best left jab in boxing. We devoted a sizeable chunk of every workout to perfecting that punch. "Let's see that left!" he would say at the beginning of each training session. I would adopt a boxing stance and flick out the jab repeatedly for his critique. It seemed that nothing else mattered as long as the jab was progressing favourably.

In those years, I often worked long hours on our farm, and at times I worked for other farmers and at other jobs. I also trapped during the winter. In spite of the heavy workload, I managed to maintain a fairly regular training schedule. Fred and I were faithful to our agreement; we were working together to build a career. Months turned into years. I gained in size and strength and steadily increased in skill. I was growing up to be a fighter. At seventeen, I was six feet tall, weighed 160 pounds, and was an extremely well-conditioned athlete eager to face the challenges that lay ahead. That fall, I left the farm for Winnipeg and launched my fistic career.

Two years later, on a trip home from the winter I spent boxing in Edmonton, I changed buses in Prince Albert and had two hours to kill, so I strolled down the main drag.

As I walked north on Central Avenue, I noticed a tall, broad-shouldered man walking toward me. He moved with an easy, confident stride that looked somehow familiar. We recognized each other at the same instant. It was Reggie!

He laughed and hurried over and, extending his hand, he said, "Kid, it's great to see you!"

I was staggered at the flood of bitter thoughts and emotions that stormed into my consciousness at that moment. A replay of that cold winter afternoon in the north hammered at my brain. I held up my hand as though to stop the flow of conversation. "Hold it!" I said. "We've got some unfinished business to settle."

Reggie's jaw dropped in surprise. "What ... what do you mean?" he stammered. "You're not still holding a grudge over what happened all those years ago out on the road, are you?"

I didn't reply.

"We're grown men now," he said. "We were just kids then. That didn't mean anything."

"It meant something to me," I replied coolly.

Reg was reflective for a moment. "Yeah, I guess it would," he said. "Whipping you that way was wrong, and I wished afterward that I'd made things right. It looks like you want to even the score today. I hope not; I know I don't stand a chance against you. I'd like it if you'd accept my apology instead, and we could get back to being friends."

As though somewhere a switch had been thrown, the dark anger that had been hidden in me began to dissipate, like air escaping from a punctured tire.

"Man, I'm astonished at myself!" I exclaimed. "I didn't realize I was full of bitterness at you all this time. You're right. Let's get back to being friends the way we always were."

"You bet!" he replied. We shook hands warmly.

As the bus rolled steadily north and east on the final two-hour leg of the bus trip home, I felt lighter and somehow more at peace. There was a sense that something that had been wrong for a long time was right at last. I sat back and thought about home. I was getting anxious to see Mom and Dad and my brothers, Harley and Dale. I wondered how Fred was doing. Glancing at my watch, I estimated that my arrival should just about coincide with the evening meal. I vividly recalled some of the great meals Mom was noted for preparing. Hmm, I thought, I wonder what's for supper?

Wilderness Trapline

A WILDERNESS TRAPLINE CAN BE A GREAT PLACE to discover what kind of stuff you are truly made of, especially if you are alone and sixteen. I ran such a trapline by myself during the early season of 1948. On that trapline, I had almost more than I could handle in terms of excitement, danger, and plain hard work. The experience had a strong influence on my life, and my recollections of the north country remain vivid.

I guess the story begins with my Uncle Ted. My uncle had been a trapper most of his adult life. He owned a large trapline in the wilderness area thirty miles north of our homestead, until he sold his line to Fred in 1944.

During the fall of 1948, Fred's poor health made him unable to handle his trapline. Fred and I agreed that I should go north in his place, at least until Christmas. We hoped Fred would be strong enough to take over in January.

Not surprisingly, my mom did not share our enthusiasm for this plan.

"My word, Son," she said. "You can't go up there alone. What if you got sick, or hurt, or lost?"

"There is an element of risk," Dad conceded, "but Lee can take care of himself in the bush. I think he can handle it. Besides, it's only till Christmas."

Finally, Mom relented, but only on the condition that Dad would take me up there and visit me a few weeks after I left to make sure I was all right.

The next week, Dad and I loaded the old half-ton with equipment and supplies and set out for the base camp on the north shore of Stinking Lake. We travelled due north. After we left the settled area, the road became steadily more primitive.

It was a tough haul for the old truck, however we arrived safely and in good spirits late that afternoon.

Dad left for home early the next morning. As the truck disappeared, a pang of loneliness swept over me. I tried to dismiss the feeling and turned to the business of getting the cabin and gear organized. I spent most of the day cutting a fresh supply of firewood.

I noticed fresh mink tracks while getting water from a spring that flowed into the lake. I returned later with traps and made a couple of sets. That evening, I made preparations for a full day of exploring, hoping to soon have a lot more traps in place.

Just after dawn the next day, I took the .22 and went to the spring for water. It had snowed overnight and the world was white and silent. The crisp air sent a chill through me and brought with it the sober realization that I was totally alone.

A flash of movement down by the spring interrupted my solemn thoughts. I froze and waited. There it was again. I moved carefully, my footsteps muted by the fresh snow. At about twenty-five yards, I knew for sure—there was a mink in one of the traps.

Just then, I spotted movement farther upstream in the spring. Another mink, a big one, was coming to investigate the commotion. I dropped to one knee and quietly worked the action of the rifle. The mink disappeared behind a rock. When the dark head reappeared, I squinted through the rear aperture, settled the front bead just ahead of his ear, and squeezed off a quick shot. I ran to the spring and found a large dark male, and twenty yards downstream, another mink held firmly in a Victor No. 1.

A few minutes earlier, loneliness had haunted me like a dark shadow, and I had felt a gnawing uncertainty. Now, I was elated. "Yahoo!" I shouted to the silent trees. The call echoed back through the spruce and Jack pines. "Yahoo!" I hollered again. It felt good to hear another voice, even if it was only the echo of my own. This was only the morning of the third day, and already I had taken valuable fur. "What a day!" I declared at top volume; a dozen voices assured me it was so.

That morning, I gave full attention to skinning those mink

A wilderness trapline can be a great place to discover what kind of stuff you are truly made of, especially if you are alone and sixteen.

and getting the pelts on stretchers. Both were dark, heavily furred, and fully prime. The larger one was exceptional by any standards. I felt very encouraged and more than a little proud of those two pelts.

A couple of days later, Harry, an older trapper whose camp was located twelve miles south and east, stopped by. We chatted a while, then Harry noticed the mink pelts on the wall. He examined them with an experienced eye. "Holy smoke-us!" he exclaimed in his thick Danish accent. "Mink, two uff dem, and dat vun, dats a mink!"

Harry said he had been trapping for several weeks and hadn't caught any mink yet. That knowledge boosted my self-confidence considerably. I had been somewhat awed at the prospect of trapping alongside veterans who had spent a lifetime in the north. Now, I felt more like I belonged in the "big leagues." Even if my early catch proved to be beginner's luck, I was not without some credibility.

I set many more traps over the next several days. Soon,

Mink and weasel pelts on the cabin wall.

quite a few weasel and many squirrel pelts also adorned the cabin wall.

Late in my second week at Stinking Lake, I embarked on an all-day journey to explore Falling Horse and Caribou creeks. Fred had given me a roughly pencilled map, and I knew that the streams ran parallel to each other. I planned to scout for animal signs and return to set traps where prospects were best. I travelled five or six miles, following the map to the Falling Horse. It looked promising, but I pressed on a few more miles to a larger stream that I correctly assumed was Caribou Creek.

I could see that a couple of moose had recently passed that way so I didn't bother to test the ice. I slid down the six-foot bank and started across.

Without warning the ice crumbled before me and was swept away by swift black water. As my footing gave way, I flipped my rifle across the creek and lunged forward with everything I had. I managed to grab the tips of some branches of a huge poplar that beavers had felled into the creek from the opposite bank. It felt like my pack, belt-axe, and sodden clothing weighed a ton. The current pulled with a force so relentless it seemed as though it was set on my demise. At that moment, the flimsy, frozen branches I clutched were the difference between life and death. Miraculously, the branches held, as hand over hand I hauled myself toward the tree. It seemed to take forever to find the trunk with my feet, deep under water. Finally, I began to gingerly climb up the slope of the huge trunk.

I had never before experienced anything as cold as the black waters of the Caribou. But I definitely was not prepared for the jolt that came next. As I emerged from the water, soaked to the skin, a stiff breeze and twenty-below-zero air temperature hit with the force of an avalanche. Searing, paralyzing cold penetrated me to my bones. I wanted to give up, but somehow I kept crawling. Finally, I toppled into the snow on the far bank.

After several attempts, I lurched to my feet. Although my body was almost immobile, my mind worked feverishly. My first thought was that I had to get a fire going. Then I made an astonishing discovery—I wasn't cold anymore. I wondered if I was hallucinating or perhaps entering a new stage of coldness where feeling malfunctioned altogether. Then, I looked down at my clothes and saw I was wearing a suit of armour—ice armour. The extreme cold had flash-frozen my outer garments, sealing out the cold and trapping my body heat inside.

I abandoned the idea of trying to build a fire. Instead, I rescued my rifle from the snowbank and struck out for camp at a brisk pace.

The trip back to camp was not easy, but it wasn't unbearable either. In fact, I felt surprisingly comfortable as I thought about the good fire I would build in the airtight heater, and a hefty pot of grouse stew.

I had no real concept of God in those days, but I had a deep sense as I trudged along that more than luck had spared my life. I was thankful.

One night a few days after my expedition to the Caribou, I was awakened at about midnight by an unmistakable sound: the plaintive howl of a northern timber wolf. Soon there was another, and another, and then a full chorus. I slid deeper into my eiderdown sleeping bag.

I had just drifted off when I heard another howl—close this time, up on the Jack pine ridge west of camp, I guessed.

Stinking Lake Camp in 1948, drawn by the author at age sixteen.

I got up, lit the coal-oil lamp, and fed a couple of chunks of dry pine into the airtight. The intermittent howling came steadily closer. "Hey," I declared out loud, "they're heading right for this cabin!"

I tried to reassure myself by remembering everything I had heard or read about wolves being afraid of humans. That knowledge provided little comfort when I heard the next mournful, chilling cry not thirty feet from the cabin door.

I grabbed my 25–20 carbine, levered a round into the chamber, and sat down on the bunk. By now I could hear wolves moving through the snow in the dry weeds and brush. Although it was cool inside, my palms were sweating as I gripped the cold steel. I kept my eyes on the window in the west wall. It was low enough and large enough for a wolf to jump through. The window had no glass but was covered on the inside with a sheet of semi-transparent waxed cloth. It would be foolish to think that a wolf would rip through that cloth and leap into an occupied cabin, wouldn't it? I wasn't so sure anymore, as I heard shaggy fur brush against the rough pine bark of the logs under the window. The hair on the back of my neck stood up. I cocked the carbine and waited.

I'm not sure how long the wolf pack hung around the cabin. After a while, they simply were gone. I could tell by the occasional distant howl that they were heading south toward the swamp country.

I put more wood in the airtight and crawled back into the sleeping bag. I left the lamp burning all night and slept with the carbine beside me, but I sure did not sleep well. Dawn finally came, and I stepped outside to examine the tracks. Seven wolves had come down from the ridge to the west, leaving tracks everywhere. One even urinated on a corner of the cabin. Was he marking his territory or just showing contempt?

Morning brought with it the renewal of my courage. I was thoroughly ashamed for allowing myself to become so fearful the previous night, and I resolved that if ever I faced such a situation again, I would grab a flashlight and rifle, step outside, and blaze away.

I heard wolves in the distance from time to time, but they never came near camp again during my stay.

Trapline life continued through the weeks. At times it was exciting, at times frustrating, but the constant was the hard work. As planned, Dad came to get me just before Christmas. It was good to be heading home, although I was sad to leave the north country.

Fred didn't recover enough to go north that winter. He was pleased with the substantial catch of furs I brought out, but neither he nor my parents wanted me to go back alone again.

The next fall, I left for Winnipeg to pursue a career in boxing. I never spent a winter in the wilderness again.

The Mad Russian

"THERE AIN'T A REAL MAN IN THE WHOLE DAMN DISTRICT," the Russian complained. "I hired three men in the last two weeks. Two quit and I fired the third one. The kid I just hired prob'ly won't last a week, either. There just ain't no men who can do a day's work in the bush."

"Tough luck," Charlie replied. "I disagree, though. There are some good men in this part of the country."

"I ain't seen 'em," the logger snorted.

"By the way," Charlie said, "who's the kid you just hired?"

"Kid named Lee," the Russian replied. "Comes from the farm a mile east. Starts Monday."

"Well," said Charlie, a smile creasing his weathered face, "you got a man who can do a day's work now."

"The kid?" the logger asked. "Why, he ain't even twenty."

"He's seventeen," the smaller man replied, "but he's not your average seventeen-year-old. He'll work with you or anybody else."

"You telling me a seventeen-year-old farm kid can keep up with me an' big George Grozny in the bush?" the Russian asked.

"Yep," Charlie answered, grinning broadly. "And I'll go you one better: I'll betcha inside of two weeks you guys won't be keeping up with him."

"Hah!" The bigger man shot back. "That'll be the day!"

Charlie just grinned. That summer I was in rock-hard physical condition. I had been doing man's work since long before I had to quit school at thirteen, and for more than three years I had been training with Fred for a boxing career.

I was preparing to leave for Winnipeg that fall to launch my career when I heard about Steve Korchinski, a man who ran a small logging operation. I knew he was working in our area and was told he might need a man or two. I also heard he worked his men extremely hard. Folks said Steve Korchinski was a wild man in the bush, earning him the nickname, the Mad Russian.

I located Korchinski on a Friday afternoon, and I introduced myself. "I'm looking for work," I said, "and I heard you might need a man."

"I might," he replied. "Can you do a day's work in the bush?"

"Yes I can," I answered.

"I pay a dollar an hour, if you can earn it," the logger said. His dark eyes challenged me.

"I've never had any trouble earning my wages," I replied.

"Be here at eight Monday," he said, "and we'll see."

"I'll be here," I said, matching his cool stare, "and I guess we will see."

That evening at supper, I discussed my new employer with Dad. "This is a strange man," I said. "He seems to be challenging me, almost implying I'm not man enough, before I've even done a lick of work."

"Who knows what his problem is," Dad replied. "I suggest you don't take it too seriously. When he sees you work for a day or two, he'll change his tune."

"You're probably right," I said. "I have to admit, though, I'm a little annoyed at his attitude."

Monday was a beautiful Saskatchewan day. I arrived at the logging site a half-hour early. Korchinski and his partner, George, were busy getting gear together. They practically ignored me.

"You'll limb trees," the Russian finally said, "and you'll mark log lengths and help me buck logs to length. From time to time, we'll haul logs to the mill site with the tractor. You and George will load and unload."

"That's fine with me," I said.

I studied Korchinski as he busied himself servicing his chainsaw. I judged him to be in his late thirties, about five-foot-ten, perhaps one hundred ninety pounds, lean and muscular: obviously an intense driven individual.

I soon discovered why they called Steve Korchinski the Mad Russian.

Big George was just plain big. He was a friendly, easygoing bear of a man. What a pair of opposites, I mused.

At eight, the workday began, and I mean it *really* began. I soon discovered why they called Steve Korchinski the Mad Russian. He literally ran through the bush, from one tree to the next. He felled the Jack pine trees with a chainsaw. I limbed them with an axe—chainsaws in those days were too cumbersome for limbing.

I was very glad that day that I was in such great physical condition. I could see that the Mad Russian expected me to run through the bush and work like a madman, just as he did.

The first day was filled with furious activity. Steve felled many trees. At first, George and I limbed together. The big man was a skilled woodsman, jovial, and fun to work with. The Russian remained surly and intense.

Well before noon, Korchinski estimated he had enough trees on the ground to keep us going for the rest of the day. He joined me in limbing, and Big George left to do some work at the mill site. Working side by side with the Mad Russian was quite an experience. I enjoyed the challenge and matched him stroke for stroke. When he ran through the bush, I ran too. I was quite sure he expected me to fade as the day wore on. I had had all I could handle by quitting time, but I didn't let him know it.

That evening, Dad and I talked about my new job. "I don't get it," I said. "This Russian is trying to prove something. He's trying to work me so hard I'll quit. It doesn't make sense."

"Are you going to quit?" Dad asked. I could see he was trying to conceal a grin.

"Not a chance!" I retorted. "He's some bush worker all right, but he's so arrogant, I just might really show him up before we're through."

For the next few days I endured some king-sized muscle soreness, especially in the shoulders. I managed to keep cheerful though and held my own with Big George and the Russian. By Friday, I had worked through the stiffness and felt great. I began to step up the pace.

We logged for the next six weeks, as summer came to a close. I adjusted easily to the gruelling axe work. Korchinski tried a number of times to wear me out. His efforts to do so always backfired, and at the end of the day he would be bushed and I would still have lots of energy.

My primary job was to limb trees. When enough trees were down, Steve helped me limb. Then I marked the trees into log lengths, using an eight-foot pine-marking pole. Steve manned the chainsaw to buck the trees into log lengths. We ran from tree to tree.

One day, as we ran, we both stepped on a down tree at the same time. The tree flipped, dumping us side by side on the soft moss of the forest floor. The Russian maintained his grip on the saw. The throttle, however, was jammed partially open. The idling chain raked into the marking pole I held in place to protect my midsection.

In a second, Korchinski wrenched himself upright and with a stream of oaths hurled the saw several yards into the bushes. "Are you hurt kid? Are you hurt?" he asked.

"I'm fine, thanks to my eight-foot companion," I answered, fingering the gouge in the marking pole.

"Dammit all!" the Mad Russian said. "You could have been ripped wide open! You know what? We're going to quit this running in the bush."

"Well, Steve," I replied, "any time you want to run, we'll run. But it always seemed foolish to me."

The Russian grunted and turned his attention to his ailing saw.

"Two more weeks," Korchinski announced one Monday. "Two weeks will give us time to finish logging this area."

The timing was perfect. I had a lot of farm work to catch up on, and harvest was quickly approaching. It was a relief knowing that this Jack pine marathon was winding down.

I had no knowledge of the conversation that took place between Steve and Charlie, before I actually started on the job, nor did I realize how important the Mad Russian persona was to Steve Korchinski. However, at this point I was thoroughly fed up with Steve's arrogance. In the final two weeks, I decided to establish who was the better man in the bush, once and for all.

That morning, I increased my work pace considerably. I knew the Russian was working at the limit of his ability.

My years of relentlessly tough physical training under Fred's professional eye gave me a tremendous advantage. I remained relaxed and cheerful, but I swung my axe with renewed fervour. The Mad Russian just couldn't keep up.

In retrospect, it must have been hard for Steve to swallow that a farm youth, thirty pounds lighter than himself, could best him at his own profession. I confess that at the time, I felt little compassion—I thought he had it coming, in spades.

Finally, the last log was hauled out of the bush.

"Well, Steve," I asked. "Did I earn a buck an hour?"

"Damn right," he grunted. "You're a good man."

"Thanks," I muttered.

"There ain't time to get to the bank today," he said, "but I'll come over tomorrow afternoon and square up with you."

"Fine with me," I replied. I shouldered my axe and left for home.

The next day, I worked a piece of summerfallow on the west half of our farm. I was cultivating with Dad's little Fordson tractor when the Russian showed up in his half-ton. I cut the switch and waited while he walked over the freshly tilled ground toward me. I felt a strange resentment as I observed his approach. It was true he had treated me badly, and at times I had been plenty annoyed. Still, I had always managed to shrug it off. Now, however, I was getting plain angry.

"Hi Slim," Korchinski said. "I want to settle up with ya and I ain't got much time."

I put one hand on the rear fender and vaulted over the hind wheel. I landed in the soft earth, nose to nose with the Mad Russian. "You worked me damn hard," I said. "In fact, for some reason you tried to work me so hard I'd quit. I can handle that all right, but if you try to beat me out of one penny of what I've earned, I'll take it out of your hide right here on this field, right now!"

The Russian's tanned face paled. "Well, kid," he stammered, "ain't no need to get excited. I expect my men to do a day's work, but I don't beat nobody outta their pay."

"Let's see if our figures jibe," I said. "What have you got for total hours?"

Beads of sweat appeared on the logger's upper lip. He fumbled as he thumbed through the dog-eared time book. "Now, I can always adjust if there's been a mistake …" his voice trailed off.

"What're the hours," I snapped. I flipped my pocket notebook open to the last entry.

"I make it 345 hours for $345," he said.

"That's exactly what I have." I was surprised that our figures were identical—I was expecting the worst.

"I ain't no crook," the Russian said. He smiled nervously. "I pay fair and square."

"Good thing you do," I muttered.

Korchinski pulled out a hefty roll of bills and carefully counted out $345. I folded the bills and tucked them in my shirt pocket.

"We square?" he asked.

"Square," I replied.

"Kid," the Russian said, "I gotta say, you're the best damn man I ever had in the bush."

"You're good in the bush, too, Steve," I replied, "and like you say, you pay fair and square."

"Gotta get goin'. Besta luck, kid!" He jogged over to his truck and roared off the field, the coarse tread of his rear tires kicking up twin showers of earth.

I fired up the Fordson, but before I shoved it into gear and got back to farming, I mused about my recent logging experience. Looking back with newfound objectivity, I began to see the humour in it. I laughed. The wad of bills in my shirt pocket felt good too, and I thought out loud, "I've got a hunch I won't ever be employed by the Mad Russian again."

Another Wilderness

It was a spring evening in 1949. I was cooling down after a hard workout, slowly unwrapping the tape from my hands. "Fred," I said, "we've got to make a decision about this, tonight. We've been thinking about it and talking about it long enough."

The small man seemed reluctant to answer. He took a deep breath and finally responded. "I hate it, but I know you're right. What you need now is lots of ring time with experienced opponents. And it sure looks like I'm not going to be well enough to travel."

"I hate it too, Fred," I said. "I hate the thought of someone else training me. I hate the thought of climbing into a ring without you in my corner. We've planned and trained for this for three years. It isn't all a big mistake, is it?"

"No, kid," he replied. "You've got something special, and you've paid the price. You're ready to take your shot. It would be wrong to wait longer."

We discussed the subject at length and agreed that it would be a mistake to postpone moving on to city rings because of Fred's poor health. The right move, we decided, was for me to head to Winnipeg after harvest that fall. I would get as much ring experience as possible and return again for fall work and harvest. We were hopeful that Fred would be well enough to accompany me to the city the next autumn.

"We've got one more big hurdle to overcome," I said. "Mom and Dad. First of all, I don't know how receptive they will be to this idea. They understand that we've planned to leave together in a year or so, but me going alone, this year? I don't know. Secondly, it might be tough for them through the winter, and I'm kind of reluctant to leave because of it."

116

"I think it'll work out okay," Fred replied. "Certainly they'll miss you, but knowing you'll be home in the summer should help. They've had lots of experience facing the winter, and they have some great neighbours."

Fred came over for supper that night and we talked to my parents together. Dad was onside quickly, but Mom was understandably apprehensive.

"My word, Son," Mom said. "You've never even visited a city as large as Winnipeg. How will you know where to go and what to do?"

"It will be strange at first," said Dad, "but he'll be able to handle it. It won't be any tougher than some of the things he's faced out here."

"But Lee's going to Winnipeg to be a boxer," Mom said. "My land, he's just a boy and he's going to be fighting grown men. I'm afraid he's going to be hurt. I don't like this boxing; I wish he'd just get a good job."

"Now, Mary," Fred interjected, "you don't need to worry. Lee's been training and preparing for this for three years. He can look after himself very, very well."

Mom was still reluctant, but knowing that I would be home in the summer won her over.

That summer and fall were the busiest of my young life. It was frustrating, too, because now that I had concrete plans to get into the fight game in a few months, I seemed to have less and less time to train.

I worked for Steve Korchinski, the Mad Russian, until the end of the summer. I got the winter's wood supply in, got the crop harvested, and completed the fall work and preparation for winter work around the farm.

On a blustery day in mid-October, I left my home on the edge of the wilderness. Dad drove me to the railroad station in Nipawin. Mom and my two younger brothers came along to see me off. It was starting to snow when I picked up my cheap cardboard suitcase and boarded the passenger car. I had a few clothes and personal things in the case and ninety-one dollars in my wallet that day. My family looked forlorn as we waved at each other through the train window. I was torn two ways: on the one hand I was anxious to get on with the course I had charted; on the other hand, I was already missing my family and concerned about how they would fare through the winter without my help.

I had more than enough time for reflection on the tedious train ride across the prairie. I arrived in Winnipeg late that night and took a room in a seedy hotel near the station.

The next day, there began what seemed like an endless succession of things to do that I had never done before. I had never used a telephone, ridden a streetcar or an elevator, let alone looked for work or a place to live in a city. These were daunting challenges for a kid from the north country. I felt awkward and a little overwhelmed—I could find my way unerringly in the wilderness, but getting to know the city was another story.

I walked east on Portage Avenue until I came to the location I had heard a lot about: the corner of Portage and Main. I was surrounded by a moving sea of people. I believe I saw more people that afternoon than I saw the entire previous year in Saskatchewan. I scanned hundreds of faces, and not one was remotely familiar. There was not one person in all of Winnipeg who I knew or who knew me.

I thought of the previous winter, when I had manned the trapline at Stinking Lake alone. There had not been a living soul for many miles. I surveyed the crowd bustling around me and concluded that while loneliness because of the absence of people is painful it doesn't compare with how alone one can feel when surrounded by hundreds. I never felt so alone in my life as that day on the corner of Portage and Main.

After studying the ads in the *Free Press* and mastering the technology of the telephone, I soon found a good room on the bank of the Assiniboine River. Two days later, I was hired on at Eaton's on Portage. Before the week was over, I went to Hallam's and purchased some boxing equipment. I couldn't resist buying a black leatherette gym bag in which to carry my stuff.

Fred had suggested that I check out a downtown boxing club he knew. I decided to look it over the next week.

I arrived early that evening. Only a few guys were there. The gym was large, and a ring occupied the far end. It was the first regulation ring I had ever seen. Several heavy bags hung from the ceiling on chains. Three speed bags were situated along the west wall. Large mirrors—used for shadow boxing—covered part of one wall. An assortment of other training equipment was positioned throughout the room. The scent of sweat and leather and liniment lingered in the air.

A heavy-set man who seemed to be in charge came over and introduced himself. "I'm Charlie Campbell," he said, sticking out his hand. He was about five nine and perhaps a hundred and eighty-five pounds. His face betrayed his former profession.

"Want to do a little boxin', eh kid?" he asked.

"Yeah, I'm looking for a good place to train," I replied.

"Help yourself," he said. "Try it for a couple of days. If the place suits you, you can pay by the month."

Charlie Campbell was friendly but not all that interested. I supposed he had seen a lot of young hopefuls come through the doors of his club.

In a short time, a lot more athletes came in to work out. The place was getting crowded and busy. I watched the boxers work. A few were rank novices. A few were quite skilful. Most were somewhere in between. However, there was one fundamental difference between me and every one of them: I had been trained by Fred Culhane and none of them had.

Fred was a masterful boxer. He had his first pro fight in London when he was fifteen. He fought in Europe, the US, and Canada. Later, he trained and managed professionals. I don't believe there was anyone on the continent at that time who was more qualified to teach the sport than Fred. I had been his pet project for more than three years, and, even though I had never set foot in a regulation ring, I was not untrained or unskilled.

I began to warm up and then moved to the heavy bag. After a while, I noticed Charlie Campbell watching me intently. When I paused, he strolled over. "Kid, you move real, real nice," he said. "How'd you like to go a couple of rounds, later?"

"Sure," I grunted. "I've been working all fall, haven't had the gloves on in months. I'll have to take it easy for a while, till I work back into shape."

"No problem," the stocky trainer assured me. "Just spar a couple of easy rounds and see how you feel."

Campbell went over and talked briefly with a sandy-haired man who was punching the light bag. About twenty minutes later he called me over to the ring. The sandy-haired guy was there.

"Kid, this here's Rod Zaleski," Campbell said.

Zaleski extended a hand and nodded.

I nodded back and we shook hands.

"I'd like you to go a couple of rounds with Rod," the trainer announced. "Gotta start somewhere, eh?"

"Sure," I agreed.

As Campbell laced the gloves on us I studied Zaleski. I guessed he was about twenty-five. He had an angular, hard-muscled body. A thin scar interrupted his left eyebrow. His aquiline nose bore evidence of many a brawl, probably both in the ring and outside it. This guy looks for real, I surmised.

Campbell motioned us to the centre and called, "Time!"

This was it! After years of training and dreaming, here I was in a big city fight club, in a real ring, squaring off with an experienced opponent.

I could see in a moment that Rod Zaleski was no greenhorn. He had moves that only come with training and experience. I felt stiff and awkward. The canvas didn't feel like I thought it would underfoot. The crude gym in Dad's garage seemed a million miles away. I wished Fred were there.

Zaleski sank into a deep crouch, moved in close, and banged both hands to the body. The jolt of his blows brought me up short. I got focused on the realities of the present—in a hurry.

Thinking boxers have an inner computer that constantly collects and analyzes information about an opponent. How fast are his responses? How does he react to a feint? How does he defend against this or that move? Can he take a punch well? What is his strategy? What strengths should I be wary of? What weaknesses should I exploit? The answers to these and many more questions help to formulate intelligent strategy while the bout is already in progress.

I flicked out a couple of light lefts; Zaleski slipped them easily. Then he threw the left hook. I got under it just in time. Fast, I noted, very fast! Gotta watch for the left hook. We felt each other out for most of the round. I began to adapt to the feel of the canvas. Before the round was over, I was sweating freely and moving easily.

Since Fred began training me at fourteen, he had been adamant about one aspect of my development. He intended

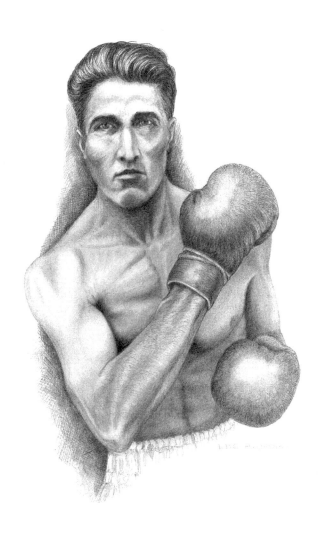

This was it! After years of training and dreaming, here I was in a big city fight club, in a real ring, squaring off with an experienced opponent.

to equip me with the best left jab in the business. That evening I wondered just how effective the left jab I brought from the northern bush would be against a seasoned city fighter. I circled quickly, feinted, then shot out the jab. "Bang!" Zaleski's head snapped back sharply. "Thank you, Fred," I whispered, though he was more than four hundred miles away.

"Time!" Charlie Campbell shouted.

In the second round, Zaleski began moving in much more aggressively. As I backed into the ropes he landed a hard right to the head. Even though I was moving away, the unexpected force of the blow drove me against the ropes, hard. No sparring here: he was trying for a knockout. Then, bang, the left hook exploded just above my right eye.

A strange icy calm swept over me at that moment. It was Rod Zaleski who had landed two powerful blows and was setting himself for the finisher. But instantly, I felt an unexplainable confidence that I was the one who was in control of the encounter. I could almost hear Fred shout, "Plant your left foot! Pivot at the hips! Put your shoulder into it!" I smashed my own left hook into Rod Zaleski's bony chin. He dangled in space for a second, then, like a puppet with broken strings, he spilled to the canvas in a heap.

"Criminy!" Charlie Campbell exclaimed. "What a left!" The trainer knelt beside Zaleski. "Criminy!" he kept saying, half to himself.

In a few minutes the sandy-haired boxer regained consciousness and managed to leave the ring with a little help.

I was angry because Zaleski had tried to KO me in a sparring session, and because I was pretty sure Charlie Campbell had put him up to it. I was mad at myself for being the dumb kid from the bush. On top of it all, my right eye was extremely painful and beginning to swell.

Campbell came over. "You okay, kid?" he asked. "Got a little bang in the eye, eh?"

"I'm fine," I growled.

"Well, these things happen, kid," he said. "Say, you didn't even get in two rounds. Would you like to go a round or two with Ramon?" He nodded toward a young man with a shock of coal-black hair.

"Why not?" I muttered. I was still angry and made up my mind I wouldn't be a sucker again.

In a few minutes, Ramon had the gloves on and Charlie called, "Time!"

For the first time I looked squarely at my new opponent. He was a chunky, thick-necked Hispanic of perhaps twenty. I had no idea what his skills were. I didn't care. I was still bristling, and now I couldn't see clearly out of my injured eye. After only a round and a half, I was already getting disillusioned with the boxing world.

We circled each other. Ramon tried a couple of lefts; I cuffed them aside. I feinted a left, feinted a right, then stepped inside his jab and ripped a short right to the head. The dark-skinned man crashed heavily to the floor and lay motionless. Blood trickled from his nose and mouth and stained the dirty canvas.

"Criminy!" Campbell muttered, as he shoved me aside and rushed to the prostrate Ramon. "Criminy!" he kept saying. "Criminy!"

I was panic-stricken. I was sure Ramon was dead.

Charlie removed the Hispanic man's mouthpiece to free his breathing. In three or four minutes, Ramon's eyelids fluttered open. Thank God he's alive, I thought.

Several other dark-skinned men climbed into the ring to help their friend. They looked at me accusingly. I felt ashamed. I wanted to leave but I couldn't get the gloves off because the laces were taped. Right then, I wished I had never left the north. I wished I had never aspired to be a boxer.

After seeing to Ramon, Charlie Campbell climbed back into the ring.

"Take these gloves off," I snapped. "I'm getting out of here."

"Hold on, kid," Campbell began, "I know things have kind of gone wrong, but…"

"That thing with Zaleski," I interrupted, "that was a set-up, wasn't it?"

"Well, I did tell him to rough you up a little," he confessed, "just to see what you had. But I didn't tell him to knock you out … honest, kid."

"That really got me mad," I said. "I should have never unloaded on Ramon like that. This is all wrong."

"It ain't your fault, kid," Campbell said. "You just did what any good fighter would do. Nobody climbs through these ropes for choir practice, you know. This is the fight game. Rule number one is: Keep your gloves up at all times. Don't ever forget it."

"Hmm … I guess I won't," I replied. "But what about the Spanish guy? Is he okay?"

"Yeah, yeah," the trainer said. "He's all right. Mind you," he added with a grin, "he'll be eating soup for a few days. Criminy, you can punch!"

I thought "criminy" was a strange word for a guy like that to be using in a place like that. I found out later that Charlie Campbell didn't use profanity. "Criminy" was one of his wildest expletives.

"Look, you've had a heck of a start here," Charlie said. "Gimme another chance. You still haven't boxed two rounds. How about going a couple with Jack, over there? No funny stuff, just sparring."

"If it's on the level, okay," I said.

"Hey Jack!" he called to a young blond man punching the heavy bag. Jack came over. The trainer introduced us. "Jack, I'd like you to go a couple of easy rounds with Lee," he said.

"I've just watched him go a couple of easy rounds," Jack replied.

"No, no, no!" Charlie assured him, "The kid only wants to spar. I want you both to promise—no heavy artillery. Okay?" We both agreed to take it easy.

"And Jack, keep away from that eye," Charlie warned, motioning to my now puffy eye.

In a few minutes, I was facing my third opponent of the night, in the centre of the ring. This young boxer looked about two inches shorter than my six feet and about ten pounds heavier. He was a clean-cut, good-looking nineteen-year-old, with the easy grace of a natural athlete. He was clever but with an aggressive two-fisted style, and he exuded self-confidence. A dangerous combination, I thought.

The first round was very fast paced. I soon established that I could land the left jab easily, so I concentrated on other moves.

Early in the second round, Jack unintentionally raked a left hook across my swollen eye. The pain was blinding.

Instinctively, I pounded a hard right to the ribs and a solid left hook to the side of the head. The blond boxer stumbled back against the ropes.

"Whoa! Hold it! Time!" Charlie Campbell bellowed. "That's it! You guys are through for the night!"

"I'm just fine," Jack said. His words were crisp and I could see he was a little ruffled.

"Yeah, yeah, yeah," Campbell laughed. "You're fine and that's the way it's going to stay."

"Sorry, Jack," I said. "It was just a reaction." I was embarrassed at having lost control.

"My fault," he replied. "I should have been more careful. I didn't mean to catch your eye."

"Everything okay with you guys?" the trainer asked.

We assured him that everything was all right between us. He grinned and seemed relieved. "Jack," he said, "cool down and hit the shower, will you? I want to talk to Lee for a minute." He threw a towel over my shoulders, and we sat down in a couple of ringside seats.

"Where did you say you're from, kid?" he asked.

"White Fox, Saskatchewan," I replied.

"Never heard of it," he said with a shrug. "Anyway, this has been quite a night. First off, you demolish two of my guys. Then, you're on the verge of levelling the best prospect I've had in the club in years, and all of this in less than three rounds! Not only that," he continued, "but in all my years in the game, I've never seen a left jab like yours. Help me out, kid; how'd you get what you got, up there in the bush in Nowhere, Saskatchewan?"

"Fred Culhane has been training me," I replied.

"Oh, I see," he said, nodding his head. "Well, this Fred is a man who really knows the fight game, there's no doubt about that. Obviously, he's been working with you for quite a while."

"Yeah, you're right on both counts, Charlie," I answered.

"So, Fred, he's your manager and trainer, then?" he asked.

"Yes, he is," I said. "But Fred is not well these days, so I'm here on my own. I plan to go back for fall work and harvest. While I'm here though, I want to get all the experience I can."

Charlie Campbell was thoughtful for a moment. "I'd sure like it if you'd train here, kid," he said. "I won't tamper with what you've been taught, and I sure as heck won't touch that jab. But, where I can help, I will. And as soon as that eye is okay, I'll get you all the ring time you can handle, in other clubs, too."

"I think I'd like that, Charlie," I said. We shook hands on it.

It had been an eventful evening, to say the least. I thought about Fred and wished he had been there. He would have been really excited! I'm sure my dad would have been pleased, too.

"Hey, Slim!" Jack yelled. "Let's shower and go for a milkshake. I've got to get my strength up after that left of yours."

"I think I need a steak," I replied, "to put on this eye." We laughed and headed for the showers.

That night in my room, I thought through the experiences of the previous couple of weeks. Northern Saskatchewan seemed a long way off. I had left one wilderness behind, but I was sure I had just stepped into another one. I had the sense that one door in my life was closing and another was beginning to open. I determined to take full advantage of my opportunities. And to remember Charlie Campbell's advice: "Keep your gloves up at all times."

I faced a lot of opponents that first year in Winnipeg, mostly in small clubs. The boxing skills I'd learned in the north were still valid in the city. I seemed to find favour with the fight crowd. They called me "the kid with the left."

One night after a fight, I was making my way up the crowded aisle to the dressing room, when a big man stepped in front of me. I found out later he was Steve Trojack, former Canadian Heavyweight Champion. "Nice fight, kid," he growled. "Say, where'd you learn to throw a left hand like that?"

"Must have picked that up at the club," I quipped.

"Did like hell!" he said with a laugh. "Nobody around here can teach you that."

It was a whirlwind year. The months slipped by far too quickly. In what seemed like no time, I was back on the farm and getting ready for another harvest.

I was very disappointed to find that Fred's health had not improved at all.

That fall I left alone again, this time for Edmonton. In the first week I found a job, a room, and started working out in a downtown fight club that catered exclusively to professionals.

A former Canadian Heavyweight Champion who managed

and trained fighters offered me a pro contract. I explained that I had a manager in Saskatchewan who wasn't well. I said if he was interested in being my interim manager until we saw how Fred's health went, I'd be happy with it. We shook on it, and I was immediately travelling in very fast company. It was another whirlwind year, and my career was advancing nicely.

I knew I was needed for at least one more year on the farm. I hoped desperately that Fred would finally be able to take his place as my manager and trainer. I decided that if his health had still not improved, I would head for Toronto the next fall.

When I returned home, Fred came over. My heart sank the moment I saw him. He was pale and drawn—obviously his health had continued to deteriorate. I guess I knew right then that Fred would never be in my corner.

"How have you been, Fred?" I asked.

His eyes fell. He was silent for a few painful moments. "It hasn't been good," he said quietly. "The doc says I'm going to be stuck with this condition for the rest of my life. We made an agreement," he continued, "but I'm not able to keep my part of it. You've got to get a full-time manager and move on without me. I'm sorry."

"Hold on!" I interrupted. "We've followed this dream for years. I'm not ready to give it up."

"Well, I'm not either," he said, "but I can't keep holding you back."

"Let's forget this manager stuff right now," I said. "You're my trainer, and you're the best there is, and I need your help while I'm here."

"What do you have in mind?" he asked. His face brightened and a flash of the old enthusiasm showed in his eyes.

"We've got to work on the left hook," I explained. "I'm looking for more fire power. Given the calibre of guys I'm facing these days, I need every edge I can get. Nobody has a left jab like mine, but I need a left hook to match!"

"Wow!" the smaller man exclaimed. "We've got some work to do. We'd better get out to the garage right now!"

We both laughed as we left the house.

"Wait a minute!" Fred said sharply as we approached the garage. "Let's see that left!"

Fifty Feet Straight Down

"IF YER NUMBER AIN'T UP—SHE AIN'T UP," Old Bill Judd said. "And if it's yer time, yer a goner and there ain't one damn thing you can do about it!"

Although I'm not so sure I agree with Old Bill's philosophy about life and death, I have to confess that in my lifetime I have been excused from surprise meetings with the Grim Reaper an unusual number of times. For example, there was one incident that happened during the fall when I was eighteen, when, like Old Bill said, my number just wasn't up.

On our farm we drew water from a well with a hand pump, as most of our neighbours did. Our water was excellent, but over time the flow of water into the bottom of the well carried sand and clay up inside the well cribbing. This buildup displaced water and hindered the action of the pump. It was necessary, therefore, to clean out the bottom of the well occasionally.

Dad and I chose a Saturday in early fall to clean out our well. Arrangements were made for a couple of men to help, however, the only one who showed up was my sixteen-year-old cousin, Merv. Dad, along with the rest of my family, had gone to town for the afternoon, thinking I had all the help I needed. Now, it wasn't that Merv wasn't capable. He hadn't yet reached his full growth, but he was already six-foot-two and weighed about 225 pounds. The kid was well proportioned and enormously strong. Nevertheless, he was a youth, albeit a youth outfitted with a big, powerful man's body.

"Well, Merv," I said. "I guess it's just you and me."

"Heck, we can handle it," he replied.

"Sure, let's do it," I responded. "And guess what? You get to do all the bull work. I get the easy part—going down the well."

"I might have known," Merv replied in his easygoing way.

We pumped the well dry, removed much of the heavy planking from the top, and positioned the windlass over the centre of the opening.

The well was a square hole, fifty feet deep. The shaft was protected, so that it would not cave in, by stout wooden cribbing from top to bottom. Ladderlike steps were nailed up one side of the crib. The steps and the cribbing remained sound, except for the top fifteen feet or so, where the wood in the top portion had gradually deteriorated, rendering those steps unsafe.

"Let the rope down and lock the windlass," I said. "I'll climb down the rope until I get to the secure steps lower down."

"Okay, champ," the young giant replied.

The descent was not difficult. I climbed down the rope about twenty feet, found the ladder safe, and went down.

It was a very strange experience, to stand at the bottom of that fifty-foot hole and look up. There was open space somewhere up there beyond that postage stamp-sized opening, but I was virtually imprisoned in a dark, damp, and cold four-foot-square world. No place for someone with claustrophobia, I mused to myself.

I began to work quickly, filling the bucket with mud. "Haul away, kid!" I hollered up the shaft.

Merv whisked the pail up quickly, dumped it, and in minutes the empty bucket was at my feet again. It probably took about half an hour to finish the job. The bottom of the well was clear, and fresh water was trickling in again. I sent the shovel up with the last bucketful, and Merv lowered the bucket one more time.

"I'm going up the same way I came down, Merv," I hollered. "I'll climb the ladder as far as I can then climb rope the rest of the way."

"Okay," came his shout. "Talk to me on the way up, though, so I'll know how you're doing."

I started up the ladder, the dangling rope trailing through the crook of my arm, just in case. As I neared the top, the steps were definitely questionable. "I'm climbing out on the rope from here on," I shouted.

"Take it careful," Merv advised. I could see him peering down the opening.

"Sure, I'm fine," I replied and swung free. Climbing rope for twenty feet or fifty feet was not really a challenge for me. Fred's boxing training program covered everything, and now I had a year in the fight game in Winnipeg under my belt. I was in superb physical condition.

I ascended the rope quickly. But as I neared the opening, a strange thing happened—suddenly, I felt dog-tired. It felt like my body weighed a ton. I forced myself to grip tighter, to pull harder, but it wasn't working. I couldn't grip the rope tightly enough. I could barely hold on, much less lift myself higher. Just as my head emerged into the afternoon sunlight, my hands began to slip. I looked in disbelief. The last image I saw before everything went black was the rope slipping through my hands. From far, far off, I heard Merv shout, "Hey! Champ! What are you doing?" Dimly, I was aware that I was falling—fifty feet straight down!

When I finally regained consciousness, I was lying on the grass about ten feet from the well. My young cousin was bending over me, shouting frantically, "Lee! Lee! What's happened to you? What's wrong? Say something!"

"I'm okay, I'm okay," I mumbled.

"No you're not okay!" he said. "What happened? What went wrong?"

Everything gradually came into focus. Groggily I sat up. "I'm all right, Merv," I assured him. "I'm okay."

"What happened to you?" he repeated, full of concern.

"I don't know, kid," I replied. "I felt great until I reached the top, then I was completely bushed. I was so weak I couldn't hold on, and everything went black. You'll have to tell the rest. I don't know what happened after that."

"Ah, well, I sort of grabbed you by the wrist and yanked you out of there," he replied.

I stood up and walked around. I felt fine, but the full impact of what had just happened was starting to sink in. "Merv, you saved my life!"

"Naw, I just did what anybody would do," he said. He looked away and seemed strangely embarrassed.

Dimly, I was aware that I was falling—fifty feet straight down!

"Look," I said, "if it wasn't for you, I'd be lying dead at the bottom of that hole!"

"But it wasn't a big thing," he protested. "You would have done the same thing. Any other guy would have done what I did."

"Hold on, kid," I said. "It doesn't matter what I might have done. It doesn't matter what someone else might have done. All that matters right now is what you did."

Merv seemed troubled somehow, that he had actually saved my life. I wondered if the young man had put me on a high pedestal because of my boxing exploits and was finding it hard to accept that I was mortal after all.

"Merv," I said, "not many guys would have grasped what was happening quickly enough. Not many guys are sharp enough to act in a split second, like you did. And certainly not many guys would be strong enough to drag me out of that hole with one hand. You did something today that most men never have a chance to do; you saved someone's life."

"Yeah, I guess so," he finally admitted. "But, I'm afraid things are going to be different between us now, because of this."

"Not a chance," I replied. "The fact is, you saved my life today, and I'm very, very grateful. I could never repay you for that. But if you think I'm going to be your slave or something from here on—forget it!"

Merv grinned.

"And the next time we have the gloves on," I said, "if you tag me with that big right, I'll pound you good!"

"Haw! Haw!" he laughed. "You mean just like always?"

"You bet!" I assured him. "Seriously, Merv," I continued, "I'll never forget what's happened here today. And I want you to know that I'm glad that when I reached the top of that well, you were the guy standing there."

"I'm glad I was, too," he replied. "I wouldn't have wanted it any other way."

For years I never knew why I had lost consciousness climbing out of that well. When I told the story to a miner friend, he explained that lethal gases sometimes collect at certain levels in a mineshaft, or a well. At last I knew that it was poison gas that had scored the knockout that day.

For a long time, I pondered why sometimes a man's life is spared from what seems to be certain death. I still am grateful for what Merv did that day, just as I was those many years ago. Nowadays, though, I look even beyond Merv's quick hand, and I am even more thankful that when I came to the end of my rope, the good Lord had His man in place, ready to reach out a powerful hand.

Bear at Close Quarters

THERE WERE ALWAYS BEARS AROUND our neck of the woods. I had no hankering to hunt them and seldom did. One day, though, I was forced into a bear hunt that went sour, and I found myself facing a wounded bear at close quarters.

I was a transplanted westerner living in Toronto in the 1950s, when I met and married an eastern girl. In 1957, my wife, Beverly, our two-year-old son, Larry, and I paid an extended visit to my parent's farm home.

It was a grey fall morning when my mother looked out the kitchen window. "There's a bear out there!" she said. "He's just coming out of the bush and he's heading for the barn!"

We rushed to the window. She was right; there in the broad daylight was a black bear, making his way boldly toward the small barn and attached henhouse.

Warning lights began clicking on in my brain. Why would a bear be so bold in daylight? Is he sick? Is he injured? Has he gotten a taste for livestock that he will take risks to satisfy? Is this a renegade bear?

I thought about my younger brother, Dale, who had walked to school that morning on the bush road less than fifty yards from the barn.

Then I had a thought that chilled me to the core. My toddler son visited his grandma's henhouse several times a day. What if he was there right now—and no one had looked out the window?

The decision was clear.

I knew Dad had his .303 Ross hanging in the next room. "Dad, get the Ross for me, and some ammunition," I said.

"The shells are upstairs," he said as he handed me his rifle.

I kept my eye on the bear's progress as I rummaged through a kitchen drawer where I thought I'd seen some .303 cartridges. I found two steel-jacketed army surplus shells. "Just what I don't want," I thought. I couldn't wait any longer, though; the bruin was disappearing behind the barn.

I shoved one of the army shells down into the magazine, dropped the other into the chamber, and ran out the door. The barn was now between the bear and me, and I wanted to get close to the building before he came around the other side.

A fine rain began to fall as I approached the old building. I hugged the wall, rifle ready, not knowing where, or even if I would encounter the black intruder. I advanced cautiously to the east corner of the barn, took a deep breath, and stepped around. We were face-to-face—about eight feet apart!

Instantly, he rose to full height on his hind legs. A low growl rumbled deep in his throat.

I flipped the safety, sighted high on the neck, and squeezed the trigger. The Ross roared and bucked against my shoulder, and the black hit the ground hard. I ripped the bolt-action open and closed. To my astonishment, the bear bounded immediately to his feet. I fired my last round at his front shoulder. He flinched but wheeled and lumbered toward the nearby bush.

I was relieved that he had not run in my direction, but I was extremely distressed that he had survived two shots that should have put him down for good. I knew now what lay ahead: tracking a wounded bear in heavy bush—the hunt that nobody wants.

I returned to the house to find the family excited. They had witnessed the whole drama. Only Dad understood the seriousness of the situation. He handed me a box of .303 soft-point, hunting ammunition. As I loaded, Dad said quietly, "Take it real, real slow."

"This is not my favourite thing, Dad," I said.

"Yeah, I know," he replied. "The more time you give him the better. He'll probably lay down soon and stiffen from his wounds."

"I can't afford to give him time," I said. "I don't know how badly he's hit, or if he'll stop at all. I have to put an end to this now, in case someone crosses his path."

Dad nodded as I slipped on a heavy jacket, pocketed a few extra rounds, and stepped out into the rain.

I picked up the tracks quickly. I found signs of blood on leaves occasionally, but not much, which made me wonder how badly he was wounded after all. It was obviously foolish to have used those steel-cased army shells.

I moved slowly, as Dad had cautioned, always ready for another surprise encounter. I tracked for a quarter of a mile, to the edge of a tilled field. The tracks led to a five-acre island of unbroken bush in the middle of the field. I groaned inwardly; the bush was so dense that visibility would be virtually nil.

I circled the island quietly and could see no tracks coming out of the bush. Now I reasoned that the bear must be hurt badly in order to hole up rather than make for the heavy forest nearby.

Bears do not see or hear especially well, but they possess an incredible sense of smell. I figured he must have caught my scent by now, which meant that somewhere in that jungle lay a wounded bear, watching his back-trail and waiting for me.

It took an hour and a half to thread my way to the very heart of the thick bush. I knew I was on track and that the quarry was close. I heard a sound—what was it? I waited ten minutes, then fifteen. There it was again, a quiet cough, straight ahead, maybe thirty or forty feet. I inched forward. Crouched there in the silence, I could hear the beat of my own heart. I was so close to that bear that I knew we were going to be face to face again, only this time I couldn't see him. Cold sweat beaded my forehead.

Now I could hear laboured breathing. The rain was deadening the sound and keeping my scent down. He hadn't detected me yet.

My attention was drawn to a large spruce tree that had blown down decades before. It rested against other trees at a very gradual slope. I reasoned that if I could climb high enough I might be able to see down into the hidden lair. I took off my boots. This was no time to snap a twig underfoot; besides, I couldn't risk slipping on the saturated bark. Painstakingly, I ascended the huge trunk. At last, peering through the dense foliage, I saw him—he was watching his back-trail.

I advanced cautiously to the east corner of the barn, took a deep breath, and stepped around. We were face-to-face—about eight feet apart!

Silently, I slipped the safety, aimed for a head shot, and fired. I slammed the Ross's heavy bolt action two more times. The three reports almost blended into a single roar that echoed through the rain-soaked trees. This time the bear didn't leap to his feet.

I waited until there was only stillness before I climbed down the tree and pushed through the tangled undergrowth to make sure it was finally over. The bear lay in a crouching position, almost hidden by heavy brush. I shivered for a moment as I surveyed the ambush I could have blundered into. Was I lucky? Did I owe my survival to hunting instincts, well developed through years in the bush? I didn't know, and I felt strangely and uncomfortably vulnerable at that moment.

I retraced my steps, found my boots, and began trudging home. I hunched against the steady rain, only then realizing how thoroughly soaked and chilled I was.

As I picked my way through the wet second-growth poplar and willows, the events of that bizarre morning replayed in my brain. The hair-raising ordeal had ended, but there was no sense of conquest, only enormous relief. "Man," I muttered, "a bear at close quarters twice in one day. Is someone watching over me, or is this wilderness going to do me in, after all?"

Lost in the Bush

THE LIGHT SNOW, SLANTED EARLIER BY A SOFT BREEZE, had turned quickly into large, wind-driven flakes. It was late afternoon and darkness was not far off. I stopped in my tracks, jolted as the truth finally hit home. I was lost in the bush.

Most folks who have spent years in the bush develop an extra sense about directions and where they are, even in unfamiliar territory. I thought that my years in the wilderness, hunting and running a trapline, had prepared me to face about anything the woods had to offer—until that late fall afternoon in 1957.

That afternoon, four of us had headed north across the Torch River. Dad, Fred, Klaus Peters (a lifelong friend), and I hankered to get farther into the heavy bush and hopefully bag a deer or two. Dad brought his venerable .303 Ross; Fred had a single shot .30–30; Klaus carried a .25–20 carbine; and I was packing a .38–55 Winchester carbine that Fred had given me many years earlier.

We had an enjoyable day in the beautiful north country but saw no deer. By mid-afternoon, the temperature began to drop rapidly and the sky lost its friendliness. Soon, there was a light snow falling, accompanied by a chilly breeze. The consensus was that we should head for the south and home.

I drove east to connect with the bush road south. Suddenly, three whitetails broke cover at the edge of the trail. They spotted the car, wheeled, and disappeared into dense bush to the north.

I stopped immediately. Klaus and I thought it was worth taking a little walk out there. Dad and Fred had had enough and elected to stay at the car. "I'll blow the horn if they cross the road," Dad said. "You'll know you've missed 'em, then."

"I'll make a loop about a hundred yards from the road," Klaus suggested. "You go farther out; maybe one of us will get a shot."

I nodded and we moved quietly into the bush. I soon lost sight of my partner but continued north until I guessed I was about three hundred yards from the road. Time to turn east and be ready for some fast short-range shooting.

The forest growth was heavy—spruce, pine, poplar, and a few willows—which, combined with the increasing snowfall and the lateness of the day, made visibility poor.

I proceeded carefully for some time but encountered no deer, saw no fresh tracks, and heard no car horn signal. They must have cut straight east, I thought. I decided to call it off, turn south to the road, and head for home. I began to hurry through the bush, expecting to step onto the road at any minute, but it just didn't happen. I increased my pace and turned farther to the right. I moved faster and farther, but there was nothing, nothing but bush.

I stopped and looked around carefully. It was nearly dark, a heavy snowfall was being driven by an increasingly bitter wind, and this was unfamiliar territory. I now wasn't sure where I was and, even more disturbing, I had no idea where I was going. The automatic inner compass that had been with me all my life was blank and silent. I was lost.

Lost in the bush for the first time in my life, I could almost hear again the quiet wisdom passed on to me by my dad years before. "Fear is deadly," he said. "It's what kills folks who die lost in the bush. If you are ever lost, the first thing you do is stop and make yourself quiet. You need to realize that the temptation to panic will come at you like a wild dog. It's a normal reaction, but that's all it is, a strong emotional reaction. To be panic-driven means sure disaster. Make yourself calm. Assess your situation carefully. Consider your best options. And, by the way," he added, "a little prayer is always in order. Choose a course of action that feels right, deep inside, and follow it calmly. Expect that you will find your way even if it is difficult and takes a long time. Never give up hope."

I was amazed that I remembered, not only the gist of his admonition, but some whole sentences. I decided to pay heed.

I examined them carefully, reluctant to believe the obvious—that these were my own tracks, and I was travelling in a circle!

I soon found Dad was right on the first count. The temptation to panic was strong. I thrust it aside and focused on assessing the situation. On the positive side, I couldn't be much more than a mile from the car—but which way?

My first decision was to make a three-shot distress signal. Perhaps my partners would fire answering shots that would help me get my bearings. I fired three spaced shots and waited. There was no reply. Should I try again? I only had six cartridges with me. The prospect of being lost in the bush and toting an empty rifle was not especially appealing. No more shots. I forced myself to stand still and be calm. I had a quiet sense deep down that I should turn right even more and proceed slowly. Hurrying was pointless. After all, I could be heading for Hudson Bay.

I turned and trudged ahead. Before I had gone a hundred yards, I found partially snow-covered man tracks. I examined them carefully, reluctant to believe the obvious—that these were my own tracks, and I was travelling in a circle!

"Lost in the bush and walking in circles," I muttered. "I can't believe this!"

Remembering Dad's advice, I stood still once again and considered my situation. I figured that I must have lost direction almost as soon as I hit the heavy bush and set a course north and west, thinking I was going north and east. In turning right a number of times, mistakenly believing I was heading south, I had navigated a large circle, finally intersecting my own trail.

Of course, the sure way to get back to the car would have been to simply turn around and follow my tracks out of the bush. Obviously, there wasn't nearly enough time before dark for me to do this; however, at the point in my back-trail where I stood at that moment, I reasoned, I could be as little as a half-mile from the road.

I took off on the run, backtracking as fast as I could. The tracks were hard to follow in the semi-darkness, but I stumbled through the bush and made pretty good time. After about a quarter of a mile, a white strip, the bush trail, showed through the trees. After a few more yards, I could see the red glow of taillights; then I could dimly make out the shape of my white Ford, idling on the trail.

I stopped one more time, took a deep breath, and, looking up into the snowy darkness, said, "Thank you," even though in those days I wasn't sure there was anyone up there or out there.

I walked slowly to the car. My hunting companions were talking and laughing inside. I popped the trunk, levered out the three shells, and carefully stowed the rifle.

Well, here it comes, I thought, I'll never hear the end of this from these guys. I slid behind the wheel. The other hunters were animated and eager.

"How many?" Fred asked.

"I didn't even see any deer," I replied. "Actually, I was lost out there and I had one heck of a time finding my way out."

There was silence for a full minute, then the laughter started. "You, lost in the bush?" Klaus chuckled. "I don't believe it! Look what all this city living has done, you can't even find your way around in the bush anymore."

"Yeah," Fred laughed. "I guess we just can't let you go out by yourself."

I laughed along with them as they rubbed it in good-naturedly. The experience was far from humorous to me, however. "I know this seems pretty funny to you guys," I said, "but what would you be doing in another half hour if I didn't show up?"

There was silence.

"Didn't you hear me fire three shots?" I asked.

"Sure," Fred replied, "but dammit, the way you shoot, three shots means a deer for sure, maybe two. We never dreamed you were in trouble."

The others nodded.

"I'm as surprised as you are," I responded. "Nothing like this has ever happened to me before. It's hard to take, but ten minutes after I left the trail I was lost and didn't even know it.

"Everything about this is so dumb," I continued, "no compass, no matches, no hatchet, only six shells, and I'm wearing a light jacket. And none of you are any better equipped. I can tell you, this is an experience I never expected to have, and it sure got my attention."

"You're right," Klaus agreed. "It could have been any of us. We're so used to the bush, sometimes we go into it unprepared."

Dad hadn't said anything, although he grinned a lot while my friends were working me over.

"You know, Dad," I said, "I remembered the lectures you gave me when I was a kid, about what to do if I was ever lost in the bush. Well, I followed your advice and I guess that's why I'm here."

Dad nodded and seemed pleased.

"I've been kind of wondering, though," I went on, "just how you figured it all out. And how did you know about the fear and the temptation to panic, and all?"

He was thoughtful for a moment, then he looked at me soberly. "You're not the only man who knows the bush and yet has lost his way in it," he replied.

The knowledge that, despite his skill in the wilderness, this had happened to my dad too was a tonic to my shaken confidence.

"Well, men," I said, pulling the Ford into gear, "let's head south before this road blows in and we all get to spend a night up here."

"Yes, by Jove," said Fred. "I've got a hunch we're in for a real blizzard tonight."

Fred was right. Later that evening a full-scale Saskatchewan blizzard swept down from the northwest, making travel in the area impossible for days.

I had plenty of time for reflection. Sure, I mused, being lost in the bush for half an afternoon is not all that serious. But, what if I hadn't made it out before nightfall? As I watched the blizzard outside, I was very thankful. That night, in the warm comfort of the old farmhouse, I made a vow never to head into the bush unprepared again—a vow I've kept to this day.

Epilogue

The preceding stories are, of course, not a thorough biographical work, but represent some experiences from an early period in my life. Many decades have passed, and a few questions were left unanswered, so I thought it fitting to add a few closing words.

In 1952, I moved to Toronto with the intention of pursuing a boxing career in eastern Canada and the US. Something was missing. In retrospect, I suspect it was finally facing the truth that Fred would never be in my corner. Eventually, I became disillusioned and abandoned the fight game entirely, which was not an easy decision.

I met a lovely eastern girl and got married.

I worked at factory jobs. At night, I took special courses to fill in the blanks in my abbreviated formal education.

I finally had an opportunity to study art. In a few years, I became a freelance illustrator.

While my art career was soon thriving, it seemed most other aspects of my life were bottoming out. At this point I had a personal encounter with Jesus Christ. It was the same profound experience that has transformed so many. I guess I was surprised to discover that the gospel is utterly true. I surrendered myself completely to the Lord Jesus and found a joy, peace, and reality of life I had never dreamed of.

In reflecting on the many times my life had been spared from what appeared to be certain death, it was not hard to see evidence of a higher power at work, though I was unaware of it at the time. I plunged into earnest Bible study.

In a short time my wife, Beverly, and I and our two oldest children, Larry and Janet, embarked on a gospel music ministry that provided music for churches, concerts, special meetings, and even radio and TV, at times.

I was asked to preach more and more frequently and soon found myself at a fork in the road, again. I elected to shelve my art career in favour of the call of God to full-time pastoral ministry—a rewarding pursuit that kept me fully occupied for many years.

Recent retirement affords the time to take up pen and brush again, to write, and still have some involvement in the Lord's work.

Thank you for taking the time to read these stories.

May God watch over and bless you, as he has me.